ZECHARIAH

Israel's Prophetic Future
and the Coming Apocalypse

DAVID M. LEVY

ZECHARIAH

Israel's Prophetic Future and the Coming Apocalypse

DAVID M. LEVY

The Friends of Israel Gospel Ministry, Inc.
Bellmawr, NJ

ZECHARIAH
Israel's Prophetic Future and the Coming Apocalypse

David M. Levy

Copyright © 2011 by The Friends of Israel Gospel Ministry, Inc.
P.O. Box 908
Bellmawr, NJ 08099

Second Printing 2013

Library of Congress Control Number: 2011941811
ISBN-10: 0-915540-82-7
ISBN-13: 978-0-915540-82-2

Cover design by Brenda Kern
Waveline Direct, LLC
Mechanicsburg, PA

Visit our website, *www.foi.org*.

Table of Contents

PREFACE

Much of today's uncertainty about the end-times comes from a failure to understand the major messages found in the Minor Prophets. No Minor Prophet excels Zechariah in its clarity and explanation of the culmination of God's program of redemption. The book of Zechariah is a quintessential prophecy that Christians and Jewish people alike need to study in order to grasp God's prophetic program for Israel in the days ahead.

There are two reasons why Christians should be interested in Zechariah. One is because of the clear prophecies concerning Jesus Christ's person and ministry that were fulfilled in the New Testament. The Messianic prophecies in the book of Zechariah are second only to those in Isaiah. The other reason is how the prophecies concerning end-times events relate to Israel, the city of Jerusalem, the Second Coming of Jesus Christ, and worship in the Millennial Kingdom.

The book of Zechariah is not only the longest of the Minor Prophets but also the most frequently quoted in the New Testament. It is obvious the prophet Zechariah wrote to provide encouragement and hope to the defeated, discouraged people of Israel who had recently been delivered from 70 years of exile in Babylon. He revealed that God had not forgotten the remnant of Israel returning from the Babylonian Captivity, and he told the nation of God's grace and covenant love.

It is my prayer this study of Zechariah will bless your heart, reveal insights about Israel and its Messiah that you have never seen in God's Word, and motivate you to share the truths found in these prophecies. It is my desire that understanding these prophecies will increase your love and support for Israel as it faces enemies determined to annihilate it—not unlike the days in which Zechariah penned these words. Lord willing, what you glean from this book will embolden you to become a voice against the evils so prevalent in our world today.

David M. Levy

Introduction to the Book of Zechariah

The name Zechariah means "God remembers." The book is the 11th and longest of what are commonly called the 12 Minor Prophets. The historical setting (along with Haggai and Malachi) is the postexilic period, after Judah was delivered from 70 years of captivity in Babylon.

Background

The book of Zechariah covers four major periods of world history: (1) the Persian period after the Persians destroyed the Babylonian Empire in 539 B.C. (chaps. 1—8), (2) the Grecian period under Alexander the Great (chaps. 9—10), (3) the Roman period (although not stated, chap. 11), and (4) the eschatological period (chaps. 12—14).

Both Zechariah and Haggai cover the same periods of time in Israel's history. They are first named together as prophets in the book of Ezra and prophesied to the tribe of Judah and the city of Jerusalem (Ezra 5:1; 6:14).

Most likely, these prophets' parents came with the returnees from Babylon around 537 B.C. Zechariah and Haggai would have been young men, growing up in Judah when the nation was indifferent to its spiritual heritage—with no interest in maintaining a spiritual relationship with the Lord. The term *young man* (Zech. 2:4) is probably a reference to the prophet Zechariah.

The events in the book of Zechariah began in 520 B.C. after Judah returned from the Babylonian Captivity. Babylon was defeated by the Medo-Persian Empire in 539 B.C. and subsequently was under the control of Cyrus. In 538 B.C. Cyrus issued an unprecedented decree that allowed the remnant of Jewish captives to return to their homeland under the able leadership of Zerubbabel to rebuild their country and lives. Under Zerubbabel and Joshua, about 50,000 people returned to Judah (Ezra 2). Zerubbabel became the governor of Jerusalem, and Joshua was the high priest.

Upon their return to the land, these Israelites were inspired by Ezekiel to renew their covenant relationship with God. For the most part, they were not wealthy, and they came to a land made desolate by the Babylonians 70 years earlier. Jerusalem's walls had been leveled, making it possible for Israel's former enemies, such as the Samaritans, Edomites, and Arabs, to come at will into the destroyed city.

The returnees were awestruck at what they found; many began to despair and grow disillusioned at their situation. To make matters worse, they possessed few resources with which to rebuild the city and Temple. Nevertheless, Judah's leaders inspired them to rebuild their altar to offer burnt offerings (3:2–6) and start restoring the Temple, with the assistance of Phoenician materials and workmen (v. 7). However, the Israelites refused to allow Samaritan volunteers to help with the reconstruction. Within two years, the Temple's foundation was laid (vv. 8–10).

Shortly afterward, work on the Temple ceased for two reasons. First, enthusiasm for rebuilding dissipated because the returnees' spiritual commitment had declined. In the 16 years that had elapsed, people put their efforts into building luxurious houses for their families, and the little resources they possessed for finishing the Temple had diminished. Interest shifted to becoming materially self-sufficient at the cost of spiritual priorities. Second, the Samaritans, who were denied a part in rebuilding the Temple, were successful in stopping further work on it. Their opposition took the form of a direct appeal to the Persian kings, Cyrus and his son Cambyses, requesting all further work be stopped. The appeal was granted, and work on the Temple was halted.

For the next 16 years, no work was done on the Temple. Apathy set in. The Jewish people showed little interest in finishing the project. Cambyses, who succeeded his father, Cyrus, committed suicide. Having no son to succeed him, his death left a political vacuum in the Persian Empire. In the struggle for power, Darius I (522–486 B.C.) put down a revolt that threatened Persia; and through his able leadership, peace returned to the Persian Empire.

Darius I overturned the Samaritans' successful appeal to shut down work on the Temple when he found Cyrus's original decree. Darius restored the decree, paving the way for Temple construction to resume.

In the second year of Darius (520 B.C.), God called Haggai and Zechariah to encourage the nation of Judah to recommit to their spiritual priorities. Haggai called on Judah to resume construction. He used such methods as the curse prophecies of Moses (Dt. 28:22; Hag. 1:6), rhetorical questions, and terse commands to bring Judah to a place of commitment and service.

Haggai's style was effective. Within four weeks of his prophecy, work resumed on the Temple. In turn, Zechariah's message provided the promise of hope to the nation by showing through his prophetic utterances and visions that God will one day reestablish a theocracy in Israel that will impact the whole world. Zechariah's message of hope and promise was written to the inhabitants of Judah and Jerusalem when the nation was again facing disaster, this time one of spiritual neglect. The Temple was completed four years later (516 B.C.). Popularly called Zerubbabel's Temple, it inaugurated what is known as the Second Temple Period. Zerubbabel's Temple did not possess the beauty of Solomon's Temple, the glory of God, or the Ark of the Covenant.

Zechariah wrote specifically to Zerubbabel the governor (Zech. 4:8), who was to deliver the prophet's message to the Jewish returnees, and to Joshua the priest (3:8).

It is clear the prophecy in Zechariah was written between the second and fourth years of Darius I (1:1; 7:1), 520–518 B.C. There is great controversy concerning the date of chapters 9—14. Conservative scholars say they were written soon after the first eight chapters, even though no date exists in the text. C. F. Keil explained the omission of dating in the last six chapters, saying the first section of the book is concerned with times of Darius I, whereas the latter section deals with prophecies in the future.

The themes of Zechariah are encouragement to complete the rebuilding of the Temple, the overthrow of Gentile world dominion, future events that will attend Messiah's First and Second Advents (as predicted in other Old Testament prophecies), and the establishment of Messiah's earthly Kingdom. Key words, such as *Shepherd, Jerusalem,* and *King,* are mentioned often in the book. Zechariah used the term *The* LORD *of hosts* 52 times and *The Word of the* LORD 14 times. Key verses are Zechariah 8:3; 9:9–10; 14:9.

A profile of the prophet Zechariah will be presented in chapter one.

The writers of the New Testament frequently quoted from the book of Zechariah. Stated Dr. Walter C. Kaiser Jr.: "There are seventy-one quotations from or allusions to Zechariah in the New Testament. One-third of these appear in the Gospels, and thirty-one are found in the book of Revelation (including twenty from chapters 1—8 and eight from chapters 9—14). Of all the Old Testament books, Zechariah is second only to Ezekiel in its influence on the Book of Revelation."[1]

---

[1] Walter C. Kaiser Jr., *The Preacher's Commentary: Micah, Nahum, Habakkuk, Zephaniah, Haggai, Zechariah, Malachi* (Nashville, TN: Thomas Nelson Publishers, 1992), 23:291.

Message

Chapter 1

There are two visions in this chapter. First there is a rider on a red horse among the myrtle trees (vv. 7–11); though Judah was troubled, God was concerned for His people and would restore their towns and Temple. Second, there are four horns and four craftsmen (vv. 18–21); Zechariah prophesied the horns (Gentiles) who destroyed Israel will themselves be destroyed by God.

Chapter 2

The third vision is of a surveyor with a measuring line (vv. 1–13), revealing that Israel and Jerusalem will be fully restored and blessed.

Chapter 3

The fourth vision is of Joshua the high priest (vv. 1–10). Israel will be restored as a priestly nation; this speaks of Messiah's cleansing of the nation at His Second Coming.

Chapter 4

The fifth vision is of a golden lampstand and two olive trees (4:1–14). The light of God's glory is to be reflected as a witness to the world through Judah's completion of the Temple. Every obstacle shall be removed as the Israelites complete the construction through the Holy Spirit's power by means of Zerubbabel and Joshua's leadership.

Chapter 5

There are two visions in this chapter. First, a flying scroll (vv. 1–4) is unrolled (30 feet by 15 feet), symbolizing God's judgment on sinful man. Second (vv. 5–11), sinners and the sinful system within Judah will be removed from the land to Shinar (Babylon).

Chapter 6

The eighth vision is of four chariots (vv. 1–8) and corresponds to the first vision. God will judge the nations that have oppressed Israel, especially Babylon. The crowning of Joshua (vv. 9–15) symbolizes the crowning of the Messiah, who will rebuild the Temple at His return. Gentiles, too, will help then.

Chapter 7

A delegation arrives from Bethel to inquire whether a national fast is necessary because the Temple is being restored. Originally, the fast was held to remember the death of Gedaliah, governor of Judah (2 Ki. 25:23–25). God used the opportunity to give a divine message to the inquirers: Their fast was neither biblical nor sincere. They should have listened to the preexilic prophets; since they did not, their prayers went unanswered for 70 years.

Chapter 8

God will restore and bless Jerusalem during the Millennium. Ten promises of blessing are mentioned, all beginning with the phrase *Thus says the* LORD *of hosts* (vv. 2–4, 6–7, 9, 14, 19–20, 23).

Chapter 9

Zechariah predicted the Lord's destruction of Israel's enemies through Alexander the Great (333 B.C.). Verse 9 predicts the Messiah's Triumphal Entry into Jerusalem at His First Coming.

Chapter 10

Prayer to God will bring blessing; but trust in idols, sorrow. The Messiah's coming will prove to Israel that He alone is the One who is able to help the nation. Messiah will deliver Israel from the Great Tribulation and fully restore it at His Second Coming.

Chapter 11

The first three verses could be either a taunt song over the destruction of Israel's enemies or a description of Israel's devastation because it rejected the Messiah. Israel was devastated because it rejected the true Messiah, the Good Shepherd (vv. 4–14), and will accept the wicked shepherd, the Antichrist (vv. 15–17).

Chapter 12

Judah and Jerusalem will be attacked by the nations of the world preceding the battle of Armageddon (vv. 1–3). While the battle rages (vv. 4–8), the Lord will return and destroy the nations that fought against the land (v. 9). God will pour out His Spirit on Israel, people will repent of their sin, and specific renewal will take place in the land (vv. 10–14) as the nation receives its Messiah.

Chapter 13

The Messiah provides cleansing from sin (v. 1): Idolatry and false prophesying will be abolished, false prophets will hide their true identities, and parents will put their own children to death if they engage in false prophesying. Israel will zealously keep God's commandments (vv. 2–6). Two-thirds of Israel will perish during the Tribulation, and one-third of the nation shall be saved (vv. 8–9; cf. Rom. 11:26).

Chapter 14

The final battle in the campaign of Armageddon will take place at the Messiah's Second Coming, when He destroys the nations warring around Jerusalem (vv. 1–3). Messiah will set His feet on the Mount of Olives and it will split apart, forming a massive valley through which the afflicted in Jerusalem will flee for survival (vv. 4–5). At the Messiah's return, cosmic changes will take place, affecting the day and the night (vv. 6–7). A river will flow from Jerusalem to water the land (v. 8), Jerusalem will be elevated and expanded (v. 10), and the curse will be lifted from it (v. 11). Israel will defeat its enemies (vv. 12–16); and, during the Millennium, the nations will have to appear in Jerusalem for worship at the Feast of Tabernacles (v. 16). Failure to do so will mean drought for the nations—or a plague, in the case of Egypt (vv. 17–19). All will be holy in Jerusalem during the Millennium (vv. 20–21).

Outline of the Book of Zechariah

I.   Call to Repentance (1:1–6)
    A. Introduction (v. 1)
    B. Indictment (v. 2)
    C. Illustration (vv. 4–6)
II. Comforting Revelation (1:7—6:15): Eight Visions
    A. First Vision: Red Horse Rider Among the Myrtle Trees (1:7–17)
        1. Month of Vision (v. 7)
        2. Man in Vision (v. 8)
        3. Meaning of Vision (vv. 9–11)
        4. Message of Mercy From the Vision (vv. 12–17)
    B. Second Vision: Four Horns and Four Craftsman (1:18–21)
        1. Seeing the Horns (v. 18)
        2. Significance of the Horns (v. 19)
        3. Scattering by the Horns (v. 19)
        4. Slaying of the Horns (vv. 20–21)
    C. Third Vision: Surveyor With a Measuring Line (2:1–13)
        1. Surveyor (v. 1)
        2. Surveying Jerusalem (vv. 2–3)
        3. Settling of Jerusalem (v. 4)
        4. Security of Jerusalem (v. 5)
        5. Scattering of Judah (v. 6)
        6. Settlements of Judah (v. 7)
        7. Savior of Judah (vv. 8–9)
        8. Song of Judah (v. 10)
        9. Second Coming to Judah (v. 11)
      10. Selection of Judah (v. 12)
      11. Silence Before God (v. 13)
    D. Fourth Vision: Joshua the High Priest (3:1–10)
        1. Choice of Joshua (v. 1)
        2. Challenge of Joshua (v. 2)
        3. Condition of Joshua (v. 3)
        4. Cleansing of Joshua (v. 4)
        5. Crowning of Joshua (v. 5)
        6. Charge to Joshua (vv. 6–7)
        7. Confirmation to Joshua (vv. 8–9)

   b. Selfish Feasting (v. 6)

   c. Spiritual Forgetfulness (v. 7)

 B. Message on Responsibility (7:8–14)

  1. Relationships Required Within Judah (vv. 8–10)

  2. Repentance Refused by Judah (vv. 11–12)

  3. Reason for Retribution on Judah (vv. 13–14)

 C. Message on Restoration (8:1–17)

  1. Return to Jerusalem (vv. 1–2)

  2. Rule in Jerusalem (v. 3)

  3. Renewal of Jerusalem (vv. 4–6)

  4. Regathering of the Jews (v. 7)

  5. Righteousness in Jerusalem (v. 8)

  6. Reassurance to Jerusalem (vv. 9–10)

  7. Rewards to Jerusalem (vv. 11–13)

  8. Repentance of Jehovah (vv. 14–15)

  9. Requirements of Judah (vv. 16–17)

 D. Message of Rejoicing (8:18–23)

  1. Fasts and Feasts of Judah (vv. 18–19)

  2. Future of Jerusalem (vv. 20–22)

  3. Favor of the Jews (v. 23)

IV. Coming Return and Reign (9:1—14:21)

 A. First Burden: Messiah Rejected (9:1—11:17)

  1. Prophecy of Conquest (9:1–8)

   a. Cities Destroyed (vv. 1–6)

   b. Citizens Delivered (v. 7)

   c. City Defended (v. 8)

  2. Prophecy of Christ (9:9–17)

   a. Messiah Presented (v. 9)

   b. Messiah's Peace (v. 10)

   c. Messiah's Promise (vv. 11–12)

   d. Messiah's People (v. 13)

   e. Messiah's Power (vv. 14–15)

   f. Messiah's Protection (v. 16)

   g. Messiah's Provision (v. 17)

  3. Prophecy of Comfort (10:1–12)

   a. Restoration of Israel (v. 1)

   b. Removing Religious Rebels in Israel (vv. 2–3)

      c. Redemption of Israel (vv. 4–7)
      d. Regathering of Israel (vv. 8–12)
   4. Prophecy of Christ's Coming (11:1–17)
      a. Place of Wrath (vv. 1–3)
      b. Pastoring the Wicked (vv. 4–5)
      c. Pity Withdrawn (v. 6)
      d. Protection of the Weary (v. 7)
      e. People of God's Wrath (vv. 8–9)
      f. Portrait of God's Wrath (vv. 10–11)
      g. Price of the Worthy Shepherd (v. 12)
      h. Potter's Wage (v. 13)
      i. Participants of Wrath (v. 14)
      j. Prophecy of the Wicked Shepherd (vv. 15–17)
B. Second Burden: Messiah's Return (12:1—14:21)
   1. The Conflict (12:1–9)
      a. Siege Against the City (vv. 1–3)
      b. Smiting the Cavalry (vv. 4–5)
      c. Sparing the City (vv. 6–7)
      d. Strengthening the Citizens (v. 8)
      e. Subduing Countries (v. 9)
   2. The Chosen (12:10–14)
      a. Spirit Revealed (v. 10)
      b. Sins Repented (vv. 10–11)
      c. Specific Renewal (vv. 12–14)
   3. The Cleansing (13:1–9)
      a. Regeneration for Sins (v. 1)
      b. Removing Sacrilege (vv. 2–6)
         (1) False Prophets Slain (vv. 2–3)
         (2) False Prophets Shamed (vv. 4–5)
         (3) Remnant Saved (v. 6)
      c. Redeemer Smitten (v. 7)
      d. Remnant Scattered (v. 7)
      e. Rebels Slain (v. 8)
      f. Remnant Saved (v. 9)
   4. The Coming Christ (14:1–21)
      a. Ruined City (vv. 1–2)
      b. Returning Christ (vv. 3–7)

c. River From the City (v. 8)
d. Reign of Christ (v. 9)
e. Reconstruction of the City (vv. 10–11)
f. Reviewing the Carnage (vv. 12–13)
g. Reverence of Christ (v. 16)
h. Religious Celebration (v. 16)
i. Rain Controlled (vv. 17–19)
j. Righteous Country (vv. 20–21)

Please note: Outline does not always follow chapter titles and outlines within the chapters.

Israel Through the Ages

ISRAEL'S PAST	CHURCH AGE	TRIBULATION 3½ years	TRIBULATION 3½ years	MILLENNIAL KINGDOM	ETERNITY
Abrahamic Covenant (Gen. 12:1-7)	Israel Rejects the Messiah	Israel's 70-Week Prophecy (Dan. 9:24-27)	Antichrist Rules (Rev. 13:1-18; 2 Th. 2:4; Dan. 11:36-45)	New Covenant Fulfilled (Jer. 31:31-40; Heb. 8:8)	New Heaven New Earth (Rev. 21:1)
Mosaic Covenant (Ex. 19:5; 24:3-8)	A.D. 33 Jesus Crucified	Covenant With Antichrist (Dan. 9:27)	Trumpet Judgments (Rev. 8:2-9, 21; 11:15-19)	Kingdom Blessings (Ezek. 37:14-26; Jer. 31:31-40; Isa. 35:1-6; 65:18-25)	New Jerusalem (Rev. 21:2—22:5)
Land Covenant (Dt. 29:1—30:20)	A.D. 70 Israel Destroyed by Rome	Seal Judgments (Rev. 6:1-17)	Bowl Judgments (Rev. 15—16)	Millennial Temple (Ezek. 40:1—47:12)	Redeemed Enjoy Eternal Life (Rev. 21:3-7)
Davidic Covenant (2 Sam. 7:8-17; 1 Chr. 17:3-15)	A.D. 70-1948 Dispersion	144,000 Jewish Witnesses (Mt. 24:14; Rev. 7:4-17)	Armageddon (Rev. 16:13-16)	Battle of Gog and Magog (Rev. 20:7-9)	Unredeemed Suffer Eternal Damnation (Rev. 21:8)
New Covenant (Jer. 31:31-40; Heb. 8:8)	1933-1945 Holocaust of World War II	Russian Invasion (Ezek. 38—39)	Beast and False Prophet Cast Into Lake of Fire (Rev. 19:20)	Devil Cast Into Lake of Fire (Rev. 20:10)	
722 B.C. Israel Destroyed by Assyria	May 14, 1948, Israeli Statehood		Christ Returns (Rev. 19:11-16)		
586 B.C. Judah Destroyed by Babylon	May 15, 1948, War of Independence		All Israel Saved (Zech. 12:10; Rom. 11:26)		
536 B.C. Remnant Restored from Babylonian Captivity	1967 Six-Day War		Gentile Nations Judged (Mt. 25:31-46)		
	1973 Yom Kippur War				
	Church Is Raptured (1 Th. 4:14-17)				

CHAPTER 1

Called to Repentance

Zechariah 1:1–6

The book of Zechariah is among the most profound in the Old Testament and of great importance in view of the times and circumstances during which it was written. Zechariah summed up and condensed most of what the former prophets wrote concerning Messiah's First and Second Advents.

His words are important not only for their Messianic predictions but also for their apocalyptic and eschatological predictions regarding the ultimate destruction of Israel's enemies and the glories that will be Israel's in the Millennial Kingdom.

The book's theme is Messiah's work of redemption and Israel's future restoration. Zechariah began his prophecy by calling Judah to repent of its sin and be restored to a right relationship with the Lord its God.

Introduction

The Jewish people had longed for liberation from their 70-year Babylonian Captivity. It came in 536 B.C. and, with it, a return to Jerusalem. It was after their return (commonly called the postexilic period) that Zechariah received his prophecy. The text reads, "In the eighth month of the second year of Darius, the word of the LORD came to Zechariah the son of Berechiah, the son of Iddo" (Zech. 1:1). Zechariah gave the exact date when he received this prophecy: October 27, 520 B.C.

Before launching into it, Zechariah provided a thumbnail sketch of his background. He simply said, "Zechariah the son of Berechiah, the son of Iddo" (v. 1).

The name Zechariah was extremely common. At least 27 men in the Old Testament bore it. It means "he whom Jehovah remembers" or "Jehovah remembers." His name was a reminder that God would not forget His commitment to Israel but would bring restoration and redemption to His people. Even today, Zechariah's prophecies reach into the future and are an ongoing testimony to Jewish people of every generation that God does not forget His promises to Israel.

The name Berechiah means "Jehovah blesses," and the name Iddo means "his time." Together they mean "Jehovah remembers and blesses in His time."

Many believe Zechariah's father, Berechiah, died soon after the family returned to Judah (536 B.C.) because Zechariah is often referred to as the son of his grandfather, Iddo, and he succeeded his grandfather in becoming head of the priestly family (Ezra 5:1; 6:14; Neh. 12:4, 16).

Zechariah was one of the returnees who had been born and reared in Babylon. After he came to Jerusalem, God called him to prophesy to the Jewish people. Zechariah's message was clear: He called the Israelites to return to God, repent of sin, and commit to finish constructing the Temple begun 16 years earlier.

Like Daniel and Ezekiel, Zechariah was given a number of visions in his prophecy. The prophet was a young man (Zech. 2:4) when he received these visions and probably continued his ministry long after the last date presented in this book (December 7, 518 B.C.). He may even have ministered into the early reign of Artaxerxes (465–424 B.C.). Age has no bearing on God's call to the ministry. Not only did God call Zechariah early in life, but He also called Daniel, Jeremiah, and Samuel when they were young.

Indictment

Zechariah began with a review of God's past anger: "The LORD has been very angry [literally "furious," "full of wrath"] with your fathers" (1:2).

God had been furious with the returnees' forefathers because they had rebelled against their covenant relationship with Him, rejected the prophets' messages to repent, and refused to stop their idolatrous practices. Yet God was now ready to turn from His anger and comfort this returning generation of Jewish people. But first, they would have to put away the sins that brought on their destruction and 70-year captivity.

Through Zechariah, the Lord extended a gracious invitation:

Therefore, say to them, "Thus says the LORD of hosts: 'Return to Me,' says the LORD of hosts, 'and I will return to you,' says the LORD of hosts" (v. 3).

The threefold repetition of God's name Lord of Hosts [armies] (used once more in verse 4) gave authority to Zechariah's message. This urgent invitation required and expected an immediate response.

The Hebrew word for "turn" or "return" carries with it the same meaning as the Greek word for "repent." Bible scholar F. Duane Lindsey made a good point when he wrote,

> *The condition for their receiving divine blessing was not simply to resume building the temple but to return to Him—not just to the Lord's Law or to His ways but to the Lord Himself. Their repentance two months before (cf. Hag. 1:12–15) apparently involved an incomplete commitment, resulting in delay in rebuilding the temple. Now, a complete return to the Lord would bring divine blessing, expressed by the words "I will return to you."*[1]

Illustration

People often try to mimic the lifestyles of their ancestors or elders, but Zechariah commanded the Jewish people not to do so:

> *Do not be like your fathers, to whom the former prophets preached, saying, "Thus says the LORD of hosts: 'Turn now from your evil ways and your evil deeds.' But they did not hear nor heed Me," says the LORD* (v. 4).

The term *your fathers* is used four times in verses 2–6, exhorting the Israelites not to follow in their fathers' evil footsteps. For their fathers either did not hear or turned a deaf ear to the messages of the preexilic prophets. They utterly disregarded the prophets' calls to repent (cf. Isa. 55:6–7; Jer. 3:12; Hos. 7:10; Joel 2:12–13; Amos 5:4, 6; Mal. 3:7).

Although permanently cured of idolatry, this new generation was in danger of giving only lip service to the Lord instead of giving Him their hearts. Zechariah's message disseminates an ageless truth that repentance must always come before blessing and that change must follow repentance. All too often, believers pay lip service to God's message and show little change in the way they live.

Zechariah warned the Jewish people to repent and not delay their decision, as their fathers had done. The prophet illustrated his point with

---

[1] F. Duane Lindsey, "Zechariah," *The Bible Knowledge Commentary*, ed. John F. Walvoord and Roy B. Zuck (Wheaton, IL: Victor Books, 1978), 1:1,548.

two rhetorical questions: "Your fathers, where are they? And the prophets, do they live forever?" (Zech. 1:5)

The obvious answer to both questions is no; they are dead! The prophet used these questions to disarm any objections the people might give to the admonition in verse 4. The returnees might have objected by saying, "True, our forefathers are dead, but so are the prophets who gave them the message. So these events have long passed and have no relevance to our generation."

Zechariah nullified that prospective argument by saying, essentially, "Yes, your forefathers passed on long ago, as did the preexilic prophets. But the words of the prophets given to your forefathers were fulfilled, and such will be the case with this generation if it does not repent."

The lesson is obvious. Israel's forefathers were evil and guilty of disobeying God's law. They turned a deaf ear to the prophets' messages to repent. Judah's destiny was to spend 70 years in the depths of a demoralizing and degrading captivity.

God gives people time to repent. But once the opportunity is gone, their destinies are sealed. Failing to respond to Zechariah's message would bring deadly consequences to this generation of Jews, just as it did to their forefathers.

Although the preexilic prophets are long gone, the words God gave them will be fulfilled:

> Yet surely My words and My statutes [decrees], which I commanded My servants the prophets, did they not overtake your fathers? So they returned [repented] and said: "Just as the LORD of hosts determined to do to us, according to our ways and according to our deeds, so He has dealt with us" (v. 6).

The curses that God's Word promised did indeed overtake the evildoers (cf. Dt. 28:15, 45). During the Babylonian Captivity, some Jewish people either had a change of mind or repented (Dan. 9:1–19). They admitted God's judgment and their captivity were justified because they had ignored the preexilic prophets and persisted in their sinful "ways" and "deeds." God's judgment is always based on the ways and conduct of His people.

The message is the same today. When we confess that we have sinned against God and repent of our sins, our restoration begins.

CHAPTER 2

God's Care for Judah

Zechariah 1:7–21

Like his contemporary Haggai, Zechariah called on Judah to finish rebuilding the Temple immediately because its completion was important to God's future blessing. Zechariah did not rebuke but used words of comfort, emphasizing God's care for His covenant people.

Zechariah's message stirred these returnees from their apathy and moved them to resume construction with zeal (Ezra 6:14). Soon after reconstruction began, the Lord gave Zechariah a series of eight night visions (Zech. 1:7—6:15) concerning God's care for Judah's present and future states. Zechariah received all eight visions in one night.

He did not imagine them while sleeping but received the divine revelations while awake. These visions unfold prophetic events that extend from Judah's repatriation to the day when Israel's Messiah will return to establish the Millennial Kingdom.

The Bible gives the exact date of these eight visions:

> *On the twenty-fourth day of the eleventh month, which is the month Shebat, in the second year of Darius [January/ February 519 B.C.], the word of the LORD came to Zechariah the son of Berechiah, the son of Iddo the prophet* (1:7).

This was three months after Zechariah's message on repentance (vv. 1–6).

The first vision involved a rider on a red horse standing among myrtle trees (vv. 7–17). The second was of four horns and four craftsmen (vv. 18–21). In these two visions, Zechariah revealed God's mercy and care for His own people and the eventual destruction of Israel's enemies.

Vision of the Horsemen

Zechariah said, "I saw by night, and behold, a man riding on a red horse, and it stood among the myrtle trees [shrubs] in the hollow; and behind him were horses: red, sorrel, and white" (v. 8).

The Men. The man riding on a red, or chestnut, horse is identified as "the Angel of the LORD"—a Christophany, or preincarnate appearance of the Messiah (v. 11). The other riders are angels accompanying Him.

It is evident from the text that the rider on the red horse stands above the others in dignity and authority. The riders stood in a ravine, possibly the Kidron Valley or other low area around Jerusalem, where myrtle trees grew.

Many believe the ravine represents the lowly or humble state of Judah, which was engulfed by Gentile world powers. Pictured here is the physical presence of the divine Messiah, who cares for His covenant people and stands ready to deliver them from the Gentile nations.

Behind the rider on the red horse were riders on horses of "red [bay or chestnut], sorrel [reddish-brown], and white" (v. 8). Much speculation exists concerning the meaning of the horses' colors. Yet speculation is fruitless because no symbolism is given for them in the interpretation of Zechariah's vision.

The Mission. Zechariah asked an angel to explain the vision, and the angel complied: "'My lord, what are these?' So the angel who talked with me said to me, 'I will show you what they are'" (v. 9).

The word *lord* is a term of respect. It in no way implies that the angel who talked to Zechariah was divine. Then the angel revealed to the prophet the interpretation of his vision:

> And the man who stood among the myrtle trees [not the LORD of Hosts] answered and said, "These are the ones whom the LORD has sent to walk to and fro throughout the earth." So they answered the Angel of the LORD, who stood among the myrtle trees, and said, "We have walked to and fro throughout the earth, and, behold all the earth is resting quietly" (vv. 10–11).

The "man" is another angel who functioned as a go-between to interpret the vision. The interpreting angel unveiled the mission of the various riders. Like a military squad sent out on reconnaissance, they were to patrol the whole earth and report back on the condition of the Gentile world. They reported to "the Angel of the LORD" that "all the earth is resting quietly" (v. 11).

By 520 B.C., peace had been secured by the Persian Empire. The

Gentile world was at rest, living in comfort and ease, free from the upheavals of war. But Judah had no rest, comfort, ease, or security amid the surrounding Gentile nations.

The Lord's Mercy. The Jewish people, who had been chastened by the Babylonian Captivity, now needed comfort. In an unusual role, the Angel of the Lord (preincarnate Messiah) interceded before God the Father on behalf of His people. This is a reversal of roles, for the Messiah's role is to represent God the Father to the Jewish people.

Here is a clear picture of a plurality within the Godhead. The Messiah pleaded to the Father, "O LORD of hosts, how long will You not have mercy on Jerusalem and on the cities of Judah, against which You were angry these seventy years?" (v. 12).

The words *how long* in the Messiah's prayer are a threefold request that God the Father would (1) remove His hand of chastening from Judah, (2) bring a speedy end to the suffering of the Jewish people after their 70 years of captivity, and (3) restore Judah and Jerusalem.

God the Father answered the Angel of the Lord through the interpreting angel. He spoke "good and comforting words" (v. 13) concerning the consolation that Judah was about to receive. In the verses that follow, the interpreting angel described the type of mercy God would bestow on Judah.

The angel told Zechariah, "Proclaim, saying, 'Thus says the LORD of hosts: "I am zealous for Jerusalem and for Zion with a great zeal"'" (v. 14). The word *zealous* implies God's all-consuming covenant love for Jerusalem and the Jewish people. This love can be compared to a husband's love for his wife, zealously protecting her from abuse by others. God's zeal includes His anger over how extremely cruelly the nations treated His city and people.

God is angry with the nations: "I am exceedingly angry [literally "with great anger I am angry"] with the nations at ease; for I was a little angry, and they helped—but with evil intent" (v. 15). The Lord is twice as angry at the nations for two reasons. First, He had used them to chasten Judah for its sins, but they manifested extreme cruelty to Judah far beyond His purpose. Second, the nations further angered God by living in comfort and ease, with little care for the conditions of His people.

The word *therefore* (v. 16) looks back to all that was said in the first vision and provides the reason for God's good and comforting words to

Replacement

Judah. God proceeded to make six promises to Judah because of His great love for the nation and His anger toward the Gentiles' cruel treatment of the Jewish people.

Promises are given to the city of Jerusalem:

(1) God will return to Jerusalem: "I am returning to Jerusalem with mercy" (v. 16). The Lord returned to His people, showing tender mercy like that of a mother's affection for her child.

(2) God's Temple will be rebuilt in Jerusalem (v. 16).

(3) Jerusalem's boundaries will be reestablished. A surveyor's "line shall be stretched out over Jerusalem" (v. 16) to fix the exact location of buildings that need to be constructed in the city.

(4) God will restore the cities of Judah and make them prosper: "Again proclaim, saying, 'Thus says the LORD of hosts: "My cities shall again spread out through prosperity"'" (v. 17). This promise is made to all of the cities that suffered when the Babylonians destroyed Judah.

(5) God reassured Judah He will comfort it: "The LORD will again comfort Zion" (v. 17). Such news was a great encouragement to a feeble remnant of returnees from Babylon who came back with little more than the clothing on their backs.

(6) God reaffirmed His divine election of the Jewish people: "And will again choose Jerusalem" (v. 17). Although the Lord rejected Israel (Hos. 1:9) and chastened it because of sin, He never removed His divine election from it or replaced it in His program, as Replacement Theology would lead one to believe. Israel's election stands unimpaired and secure.

These promises were partially fulfilled in Zechariah's day. But a greater fulfillment awaits the return of Israel's Messiah, when He will judge Israel's enemies and bring to full fruition the six promises He made to it.

Vision of the Horns

Zechariah lifted up his eyes and saw another vision, this time four horns (Zech. 1:18). He asked the interpreting angel, "What are these?" (v. 19).

The angel answered, "These are the horns that have scattered Judah, Israel, and Jerusalem" (v. 19). The word *horn* in Scripture speaks of a nation's or individual's invincible power. It often symbolizes Gentile empires (Dan. 7:24; Rev. 17:12) that oppose Judah. Although the Bible does not state whom the four horns represent, many commentators see them as Babylon, Medo-Persia, Greece, and Rome (Dan. 2; 7—8). The Jewish people were severely brutalized and scattered under the savagery of these nations.

Within the vision, Zechariah also saw "four craftsmen [smiths]" (Zech. 1:20), workers who were skilled in shaping materials from wood, stone, and metal. The prophet asked, "What are these coming to do?" (v. 21).

The interpreting angel answered, "The craftsmen are coming to terrify them [the horns], to cast out the horns of the nations that lifted up their horn against the land of Judah to scatter it" (v. 21). The craftsmen will terrify (strike fear in) and destroy the horns that severely persecuted, destroyed, or scattered Judah. Although the craftsmen are not identified, they probably represent each subsequent empire that succeeded in overthrowing the one before it. In other words, Medo-Persia overthrew Babylon; Greece under Alexander the Great captured the Persian Empire; the Roman Empire took over the Macedonian-Greek Empire after Alexander the Great died and his kingdom disintegrated; and the Roman Empire, to be revived just before the Tribulation, is destined to be destroyed by the Messiah at His Second Coming. Then the Messiah's Millennial Kingdom will fill the whole earth (Dan. 2:34–35, 44–45; Rev. 19:16—20:6). God has promised Israel, "No weapon formed against you shall prosper" (Isa. 54:17).

The Jewish people today can take great comfort in these promises of God's care and preservation, knowing that Israel will never suffer annihilation by any nation (Jer. 30:11).

CHAPTER 3

Jerusalem's Future Glory

Zechariah 2:1–13

No city is more treasured by the Lord than Jerusalem. The prophet Ezekiel said Jerusalem is set in the middle of the nations (Ezek. 5:5), and the prophet Ahijah called Jerusalem "the city which I have chosen for Myself, to put My name there" (1 Ki. 11:36).

Likewise, there is no place on earth that fills the Jewish heart with love and loyalty like the city of Jerusalem. Jewish exiles have prayed for centuries, "If I forget you, O Jerusalem, let my right hand forget its skill! If I do not remember you, let my tongue cling to the roof of my mouth—if I do not exalt Jerusalem above my chief joy" (Ps. 137:5–6).

In chapter two, Zechariah recorded another vision he received from the Lord concerning the city of Jerusalem. This vision not only describes Jerusalem's reconstruction after the Babylonian Captivity but also foreshadows Jerusalem's reconstruction in the Millennial Kingdom.

Surveying Jerusalem

Zechariah said, "I raised my eyes and looked, and behold, a man with a measuring line in his hand" (Zech. 2:1). The phrase *I raised my eyes* indicates the prophet was experiencing a new vision, the third of eight received in one night. The measuring line was not just any line. The Hebrew indicates it was a surveyor's line.

Zechariah inquired concerning the vision, "Where are you going?" (v. 2). The man replied, "To measure Jerusalem, to see what is its width and what is its length" (v. 2). Jerusalem was being surveyed in order to plan its restoration.

Who is the man? He cannot be the angel who spoke with the prophet in verse 3 or the "young man" in verse 4. Some commentators identify him simply as an Israelite with the occupation of a surveyor, but we know he is more than a mere man. Others see him as an angel charged with measuring Jerusalem.

Still others believe he is the Angel of the Lord, Israel's Messiah. For in the second vision the man (1:8, 10) who appears to Zechariah is divine and identified as "the Angel of the Lord" (vv. 11–12). The same can be said of the man called "The Branch" in the eighth vision (6:12–13). Furthermore, Ezekiel prophesied of a man with a similar mission (Ezek. 40:3) who also is divine (43:6–7).

Although Scripture does not identify the surveyor, other passages would lead one to believe that He is the divine Messiah of Israel.

Settling Jerusalem

While Zechariah was receiving the surveyor's answer, the interpreting angel who spoke with the prophet left to meet another angel who had a revelation from God. Zechariah reported what happened:

And there was the angel who talked with me, going out; and another angel was coming out to meet him, who said to him, "Run, speak to this young man, saying: 'Jerusalem shall be inhabited as towns without walls, because of the multitude of men and livestock in it. For I,' says the LORD, 'will be a wall of fire all around her, and I will be the glory in her midst'" (Zech. 2:3–5).

The interpreting angel tells the latter angel to give God's revelation to the "young man" (Zechariah). He is to run, or make haste, because of its urgency and the thrilling news of Jerusalem's reconstruction. This news would fill both Zechariah and the residents of Jerusalem with great joy, for it was coming when the Israelites were struggling to rebuild their city and Temple.

God gave Zechariah four promises in the third vision:

(1) **Prosperity**. First, Jerusalem will experience prosperity: "Jerusalem shall be inhabited as towns without walls, because of the multitude of men and livestock in it" (v. 4). The Hebrew word for "inhabited" means "to expand or overflow the bounds of the city or village" in contrast to a walled city.

Thus Jerusalem would be much larger when rebuilt because of increased population, reconstruction, and material wealth. The ultimate fulfillment of this prophecy will take place in the Millennial Kingdom when Jerusalem becomes the capital of the world.

(2) Protection. Second, Jerusalem will experience divine protection: "'For I,' says the LORD, 'will be a wall of fire all around her, and I will be the glory in her midst'" (v. 5). This is a personal word from the Lord that He and He alone will be the city's divine Protector. The Lord will be a "wall" (i.e., ring of fire) around His people, protecting them from men or wild animals that try to hurt them. This is the greatest assurance and defense any people could be given.

Moreover, the Lord declared that He will be "the glory" in the midst of Jerusalem. This is none other than a promise of God's Shekinah (personal) glory that once filled the Holy of Holies in the Tabernacle and Temple. The glory that had departed (Ezek. 11:22–23) will return to Jerusalem.

Ezekiel prophesied the Shekinah will dwell in the future Millennial Temple (43:1–5). Zechariah's prophecy more fully revealed the function of God's glory. In Temple days, only the high priest was able to get a glimpse of the Shekinah glory; but during the Millennium, the Lord will unveil His glory continually to all who dwell in Jerusalem. The ultimate fulfillment of this prophecy will be seen in the New Jerusalem (Rev. 21:23).

(3) Population. Jerusalem's population will be greatly multiplied. The Lord called His people home:

"Up, up! Flee from the land of the north," says the LORD; "for I have spread you abroad like the four winds of heaven," says the LORD. "Up, Zion! Escape, you who dwell with the daughter of Babylon" (Zech. 2:6–7).

The majority of Jewish people had chosen to remain in Babylon when the Lord made a way for them to be repatriated to Jerusalem; now they are encouraged to return to Jerusalem. The prophecy also looks forward to a day when God will call Israel back to its land after the Messiah's Second Coming.

(4) Punishment. The nations who plundered and destroyed Israel will be punished:

For thus says the LORD of hosts: "He [God the Father] sent Me [the Servant of the Lord] after glory, to the nations which plunder you. . . .For surely I will shake My hand against them, and they shall become spoil for their servants. Then you will know that the LORD of hosts has sent Me" (vv. 8–9).

In other words, the prophecy foresees the day when God the Father will send the Messiah in His First and Second Comings to manifest His glory and, at His Second Coming, bring judgment on Israel's enemies (cf. Isa. 61:2–3; Lk. 4:17–19). Part of bringing glory to God will be to punish and plunder Israel's enemies and reestablish Israel in its own land. When Israel's kingdom is restored, the nation will be exalted above its enemies, who will become Israel's servants.

In that day, Israel and the world will know that God the Father sent the Angel of the Lord—Messiah—to accomplish all of this. In so doing, the Messiah will prove God's love and faithfulness in keeping His promises to Israel. When all of this takes place, God's glory will be displayed through His wisdom and character.

Jewish people are extremely precious to God. This fact is seen in Zechariah 2:8: "For he who touches you touches the apple [gate] of His [God's] eye" (cf. Dt. 32:10; Ps. 17:8). The word *apple* speaks of the aperture or pupil in the iris of the eye that allows light to reflect images on the eye's retina. The pupil is highly tender and sensitive and must be guarded from contact with any foreign object that could injure the eye. In like manner, Jewish people are precious in God's sight and must be guarded from injury. The Lord is highly sensitive to any individual or nation that would mistreat or harm Israel. He feels the injury to Israel as if it were done to Him, and He will bring a divine curse on all individuals and nations who harm the Jewish people (Gen. 12:3).

Singing in Jerusalem

The inhabitants of Jerusalem are told to praise God and rejoice over their future for three reasons.

(1) God's Presence. The Savior will dwell in Jerusalem: "'Sing and rejoice, O daughter of Zion! For behold, I am coming and I will dwell in your midst,' says the LORD" (Zech. 2:10).

The word *dwell* is the root word for "Shekinah," indicating the Lord's presence. Messiah will fulfill this prophecy when He takes up residence in Jerusalem and reigns from the throne of David.

(2) Gentiles' Position. People from every nation will come to know the Lord and be joined to Him:

Many nations shall be joined to the LORD in that day, and they shall become My people. And I will dwell in your midst. Then you will know that the LORD of hosts has sent Me to you (v. 11).

Gentiles who trust in the Lord will come from every nation to worship the Messiah when He rules and reigns in Jerusalem (Isa. 2:2–3; Mic. 4:1).

(3) Judah's Privilege. Judah will be uniquely privileged: "And the LORD will take possession of Judah as His inheritance in the Holy Land, and will again choose Jerusalem" (Zech. 2:12). The massive conversion of Gentiles might lead one to believe God's promises to Israel have been annulled or abrogated. But nothing can be further from the truth.

Israel's election is unconditional and irrevocable. Here God reaffirms His covenant commitment and again declares Israel and Jerusalem as His portion and inheritance (cf. Dt. 4:20; 9:26; 32:9; Isa. 19:25). The phrase *will again choose Jerusalem* does not mean the Lord has elected Israel a second time but only that He reaffirmed His original choice.

Zechariah 2:12 is the only place where the phrase *Holy Land* appears in the Bible. It is wrong to designate the land as holy today. The land will not be holy until Israel's sin is removed at the Messiah's Second Coming (3:9; 13:1). Then Israel will be called "the holy people" (Isa. 62:12) and be made His priests and servants (61:6). These prophecies will be fulfilled in the Millennium (Zech. 14:20–21).

Silence Before Jehovah

Zechariah called on all men to pause and contemplate in silent awe the glorious revelation that was given: "Be silent, all flesh, before the LORD, for He is aroused [awakened] from His holy habitation [dwelling]!" (2:13).

This verse does not mean the Lord is asleep but that He is incited to act in bringing God's program to fruition. So awesome are Messiah's coming judgment on the wickedness of Gentile nations and His future blessing to Israel in a reconstructed Jerusalem that the whole earth is admonished to be hushed at this prospect.

CHAPTER 4

Israel's Cleansing

Zechariah 3:1–10

Zechariah's call to repentance (Zech. 1:1–6) indicated the returnees were not spiritually prepared for their new life in Jerusalem. It was not enough for Israel to be restored to its land; it needed to be cleansed from the Babylonian culture and defilement of sin in order to experience total restoration and renewed communion with God. Israel's cleansing is the theme of vision four.

Vision four is unlike the first three visions. In the first three, Zechariah asked questions because there was an interpreting angel to answer them. Vision four contains no questions and no interpreting angel. Instead, the meaning of this vision is revealed as the text unfolds.

Joshua's Condemnation

The vision opened with Zechariah witnessing a trial in the court of heaven. Three figures were present. The prophet wrote, "Then he showed me Joshua the high priest standing before the Angel of the LORD, and Satan standing at his right hand to oppose him" (3:1).

The Person Accused Was Joshua. Joshua was Israel's high priest. He journeyed with Zerubbabel in the first wave of returns from Babylon and was presented as standing before the Lord, which, for a high priest, was the place of service.

However, before a high priest can minister, he must be ritually clean (Lev. 21:10–15). In this court scene, Joshua stood before the Lord "clothed with filthy garments" (Zech. 3:3). Actually, they were covered with excrement, the vilest type of uncleanness. Such defilement made Joshua ritually unclean and disqualified him to function as Israel's high priest before the Lord.

No specific charge was brought against Joshua. But the priest's filthy garments represented both his and Israel's unclean state. Like Joshua, sinful Israel must be cleansed and reinstated to its priestly office before God can dwell in the midst of Jerusalem (2:10).

The Prosecuting Attorney Was Satan. Satan stood at Joshua's right hand, ready to resist or accuse him (3:1). The right hand was the traditional place an accuser stood in a Jewish court of law. In Hebrew, *Satan* means "adversary" or "accuser." Although he was pictured as standing ready to accuse Joshua, no accusation appears in the text.

Satan has access to God's throne, where he accuses God's people day and night (Job 1—2; Rev. 12:10). Likewise, in his zeal to charge Joshua with sin, Satan charged Israel as well. He stood ready to reveal Israel as unworthy of God's elective calling and blessing.

Satan's evidence against both Joshua and Israel was indisputable before the court of a holy and just God. Yes, Satan was right. Joshua and Israel were guilty of sin and worthy of judgment. Satan would rest his case, confident of a guilty verdict, if it were not for God's grace. It has been rightly said, "When Satan talks to us about God, he lies, but when he talks to God about us, he tells the truth!"[1]

The Personal Advocate for Israel Was the Lord. The Angel of the Lord, the personal advocate for Israel, answered the accuser: "And the LORD said to Satan, 'The LORD rebuke you, Satan! The LORD who has chosen Jerusalem rebuke you! Is this not a brand plucked from the fire?'" (Zech. 3:2).

The word *LORD* appears three times in verse 2 but applies to two persons. The first *LORD* is "the Angel of the Lord," who has already been identified as the preincarnate Christ (1:11–12). He is a different person from the *LORD* who rebukes Satan. That word *LORD* refers to God the Father. God administered the rebuke directly, decisively, incisively, sternly, and with finality. The rebuke is mentioned twice to enforce its meaning.

God's elective grace and purposes for Israel take precedence over any accusation or attack Satan might bring against the nation. Divine, unmerited grace is the only basis for the Lord's election of Israel (Dt. 7:6–11). The Lord's grace and covenant relationship with Israel guarantee the nation will survive Satan's continual attempts to annihilate it as long as the earth exists (Jer. 31:35–37).

God substantiates Israel's survival by posing a rhetorical question: "Is this not a brand plucked from the fire?" (Zech. 3:2). Pulling a burning

---

[1] Warren W. Wiersbe, *Be Heroic* (Colorado Springs, CO: Victor Books, 1997), 98.

branch from a fire rescues it from complete consumption. Israel has often been delivered from destruction: the Egyptian captivity (Dt. 4:20); the Assyrian invasion of the 10 northern tribes (Amos 4:11); the Babylonian Captivity (Isa. 48:10); and, in the future, the Great Tribulation (Zech. 13:9). God promises to defend and deliver Israel from all its enemies, especially Satan. Israel, like the burning bush in Exodus 3, will go through the fires of affliction but will never be consumed.

Joshua's Cleansing

Standing before the court in loathsome garments stained with excrement, Joshua and Israel were unworthy of God's mercy, defense, acquittal, and blessing. Both stood helplessly condemned in sin, unable to defend or deliver themselves.

Then Israel's advocate, the Angel of the Lord, addressed Joshua's uncleanness:

Now Joshua was clothed with filthy garments, and was standing before the Angel. And He answered and spoke to those who stood before Him, saying, "Take away the filthy garments from him." And to him He said, "See, I have removed your iniquity from you, and I will clothe you with rich robes." And I said, "Let them put a clean turban on his head." So they put a clean turban on his head, and they put the clothes on him. And the Angel of the LORD stood by (3:3–5).

At the Lord's command, angels removed Joshua's soiled garments and replaced them with clean, rich, festive robes—a symbol of purity and righteousness. Zechariah, caught up in the thrilling prophecy, boldly interrupted the proceeding: "Let them put a clean turban on his [Joshua's] head" (v. 5).

The glistening, clean turban was a large head-wrap worn by the high priests. Tied on it was a gold plate engraved with the words *HOLINESS TO THE LORD* (Ex. 28:36–38). Placing the turban on Joshua's head was symbolic of his moral and spiritual cleansing, making him fit to be reinstated as Israel's high priest. It also symbolizes Israel's future cleansing and reinstatement as "priests" and "servants" of God (Isa. 61:6; cf. Ex. 19:6) in the Millennial Kingdom. The Angel of the Lord (preincarnate Christ) stood by, blessing the procedure.

Joshua's Charge

The Lord charged Joshua concerning his obedience and faithfulness:

Then the Angel of the LORD admonished Joshua, saying,
"Thus says the LORD of hosts: 'If you will walk in My ways,
and if you will keep My command, then you shall also judge
My house, and likewise have charge of My courts; I will give
you places to walk among these who stand here'" (Zech.
3:6–7).

Three divine blessings were promised to Joshua if he fulfilled two conditions spoken in this charge. The first condition was to "walk in My [God's] ways." Joshua was to conduct himself in keeping with the Lord's commandments. The second condition was "to keep My [God's] command," or faithfully perform his priestly service with fidelity to the Lord. Then Joshua would enjoy three blessings: He would be a ruler of God's Temple; be a protector of the Temple from idolatry and ungodly practices; and, like the angels, have access to God.

Joshua's Cleansing Confirmed

God Himself addressed Joshua and his fellow priests with a long-awaited announcement:

Hear, O Joshua, the high priest, you and your companions
who sit before you, for they are a wondrous sign; for behold,
I am bringing forth My Servant, the BRANCH (v. 8).

"Hear" indicates this message was extremely important and worthy of full attention. The men sitting with Joshua are "a wondrous sign"; that is, they are a sign or foreshadowing of Israel's future conversion, cleansing, and ministry.

When will this great transformation take place? It will occur at Messiah's Second Coming when He redeems Israel and cleanses it from sin. Three Messianic terms are used to describe the Messiah, who will bring cleansing to Israel.

First, He is called "My Servant" (v. 8). Christ is clearly identified as the Servant of the Lord who came to do the Father's will by redeeming mankind (Isa. 42:1; 49:3–4; 50:10; 52:13; 53:11).

Second, He is called "the BRANCH" (Zech. 3:8). The word *Branch* is a proper name for the Messiah and is used by Zechariah (cf. 6:12) and Jeremiah (Jer. 23:5–6) in this way. Messiah, "the Branch," will remove

Israel's iniquities and bring cleansing to the nation at His Second Coming. More will be said of Christ the Branch in chapter six.

Third, He is called "the Stone." Zechariah describes the Stone and its application:

"For behold, the stone that I have laid before [held out to] Joshua: upon the stone are seven eyes. Behold, I will engrave its inscription," says the LORD of hosts, "and I will remove the iniquity of that land in one day" (Zech 3:9).

Throughout Scripture the Messiah is seen as a stone of stumbling (Isa. 8:14; Rom. 9:32–33), rejected stone (Ps. 118:22–23; Mt. 21:42), smitten stone (Ex. 17:6; 1 Cor. 10:4), smiting stone at His Second Coming (Dan. 2:34–35), and the cornerstone (Ps. 118:22–23; Mt. 21:42).

Evidence is provided by God the Father to confirm that the stone refers to the Messiah: (1) The "seven eyes" on the stone denote His infinite intelligence and omniscience (Isa. 11:2; Zech. 4:10; Rev. 5:6). (2) The engraving on the stone is not revealed, but the statement must have something to do with the Messiah's future removal of Israel's iniquity. (3) The sentence "I will remove the iniquity of that land in one day" refers to Israel's redemption at the Messiah's Second Coming. God will pour out His Spirit on the people of Israel, and they will repent bitterly over their sin and be saved (Zech. 12:10—13:1; Rom. 11:25–27).

The phrase *in that day* (Zech. 3:10) is eschatological. It pictures the time when Israel will experience peace, prosperity, and productivity in the Messianic Age. Neighbors sitting under the "vine and under [the] fig tree" (v. 10) speak of the peace and contentment that will characterize this period.

God's divine purpose for Israel continues to be immutable and secure. In that day, Israel will be like a burning branch rescued from the fire of annihilation. It will be cleansed from sin, clothed in righteousness, and forged into a Kingdom of priests that will minister to the world.

This revelation of God's faithfulness to Israel gave Zechariah and Joshua hope and encouragement. In every age, Jewish people who anticipate the Messiah's return and reign can likewise take hope in His promises. God has kept, and will keep, His promises to Israel.

CHAPTER 5

Serving in God's Spirit

Zechariah 4:1–14

The official seal for the State of Israel, unveiled on February 10, 1949, consists of a seven-branched menorah (lampstand/candelabra) with an olive branch on either side. Opposite the entrance to the Israeli Knesset (parliament) stands a great menorah with branches that reach 16 feet high and 13 feet wide. This particular menorah is decorated with figures highlighting Israel's history and engraved with the Scripture "'Not by might nor by power, but by My Spirit,' says the LORD of hosts."

The menorah, olive branches, and inscription are symbols of the rebirth of the State of Israel—a graphic reminder and witness of God's power and promise to preserve the Jewish people.

The inspiration for both Israel's seal and the inscription on the giant menorah was taken from Zechariah's fifth vision in chapter 4. These same symbols that inspired modern-day Israel were first used centuries earlier to inspire Zerubbabel to finish construction of the second Temple.

Zechariah's Revelation

Zechariah began his fifth vision by relaying the revelation he received from the interpreting angel:

> *Now the angel who talked with me came back and wakened me, as a man who is wakened out of his sleep. And he said to me, "What do you see?" So I said, "I am looking, and there is a lampstand of solid gold with a bowl on top of it, and on the stand seven lamps with seven pipes to the seven lamps. Two olive trees are by it, one at the right of the bowl, and the other at its left"* (Zech. 4:1–3).

Most likely, Zechariah was not asleep as we know it but in a state of spiritual exhaustion or trauma, overwhelmed by the previous four visions that had come to him in quick succession (cf. Dan. 10:8–9).

When the interpreting angel asked Zechariah what he saw, the prophet answered, "a lampstand of solid gold" (Zech. 4:2). Zechariah described a lampstand that was entirely different from the one standing in the Tabernacle. First, he saw a "bowl [container] on top" of it filled with olive oil that flowed to seven lamps. Second, the container had seven tubes connected to each lamp. In Hebrew, the text "seven pipes to the seven lamps" reads "seven and seven," meaning seven pipes were connected to each lamp, making a total of 49 tubes, which allowed oil to flow directly to the lamp without the assistance of a priest. Third, an olive tree is pictured on each side of the lampstand, supplying oil directly to the container through "two gold pipes" (v. 12). The olive oil is described as "golden oil," or yellow in color (v. 12).

The lampstand provided light in the holy place so that the priest could see as he ministered. A lighted lampstand also represented the nation of Israel as the Lord's chosen witness to bring spiritual light to a world living in pagan darkness.

Zechariah asked the interpreting angel, "What are these, my lord?" (v. 4).

The angel answered the question with a question: "Do you not know what these are?"

Zechariah responded, "No, my lord" (v. 5). The angel's question intimated that Zechariah, who as a priest as well as prophet, should have understood what he saw. The question is not answered until the end of the chapter.

Zerubbabel Rebuilds

The angel continued to give Zechariah further revelation: "This is the word of the LORD to Zerubbabel: 'Not by might nor by power, but by My Spirit,' says the LORD of hosts" (v. 6). Zerubbabel, who had laid the foundation of the second Temple 16 years earlier, was assured he would complete the task, but not by might (human strength, wisdom, wealth, or military force) or by any human power. The insurmountable difficulties in completing the construction could be overcome only by the power of God's Spirit. A finished Temple would provide irrefutable evidence to Zechariah and Zerubbabel that God's Spirit alone, not Israel, accomplished the task.

The angel revealed that Zerubbabel would face great obstacles and opposition:

> *Who are you, O great mountain? Before Zerubbabel you*
> *shall become a plain! And he shall bring forth the capstone*
> *with shouts of "Grace, grace to it!" (v. 7).*

The word *who* was used to personify the phrase *great mountain,* which was a metaphor for the obstacles and opposition that confronted Zerubbabel. He started to rebuild the Temple after the Jewish remnant had returned to Jerusalem (cf. Ezra 3:8), and he immediately faced what seemed to be insurmountable problems.

Gentiles living in the land tried to stop the Temple reconstruction. (See Ezra 4:1–24.) First, they wanted to help with the task but were rejected because they did not follow the God of Israel. Making an ungodly alliance with these people would have diverted Israel and weakened the Jewish nation's resolve to finish the project. Then those Gentiles tried to discourage and intimidate the workers by hiring counselors to frustrate construction. Finally, those opposing the project wrote letters of complaint to King Artaxerxes, petitioning him to shut down the project. Nevertheless, this seeming mountain of opposition would "become a plain," or be leveled by the Lord, so that Zerubbabel's Temple could be expeditiously completed.

And it was completed when Zerubbabel finished it off with a "capstone" (Zech. 4:7). This was not the foundation stone laid 16 years earlier. It was the "top stone," or last stone, put in place to complete the Temple. When Zerubbabel set the capstone in place, shouts of "grace, grace to it" (v. 7) could be heard echoing throughout Jerusalem. The word *grace* can be interpreted as a request for God to bless the worship place with His favor, or it could be interpreted as the people praising God for His favor in restoring the beautiful Temple for Israel.

Zechariah's confidence in the Temple's completion received a boost by an encouraging word of assurance from the interpreting angel. The prophet wrote,

> *Moreover the word of the LORD came to me, saying: "The*
> *hands of Zerubbabel have laid the foundation of this temple;*
> *his hands shall also finish it. Then you will know that the*
> *LORD of hosts has sent Me to you" (vv. 8–9).*

These verses are not a repeat of verse 7 but an emphatic announcement that what Zerubbabel had begun, he would finish. This encouragement came from the "LORD of hosts" (Jehovah of armies), a phrase used by the postexilic prophets to describe an all-powerful God who will accomplish what He decrees.

Great hope filled the elders of Judah, who envisioned a Temple possessing the glories they had gazed on before their captivity. But as the walls went up, people's spirits came down. Those who had not seen the grandeur of Solomon's Temple praised the Lord. But the older generation, who lived before the destruction of Solomon's Temple, wept loudly and profusely because Zerubbabel's Temple was nothing in comparison to Solomon's. They scorned the new structure as insignificant compared to the first Temple because it was small and plain.

Zechariah silenced the critics with a word from God: "For who has despised the day of small things?" (v. 10). The Lord rebuked those who scorned. Nothing God commissions to be built for His glory should be considered insignificant. God often uses so-called "small" people and places to accomplish great projects.

As the Temple went up, the nation's attitude changed from one of criticism to rejoicing. Zechariah wrote,

For these seven rejoice to see the plumb line in the hand of Zerubbabel. They are the eyes of the LORD, which scan to and fro throughout the whole earth (v. 10).

The plumb line in Zerubbabel's hand was to assure proper alignment of the stones as Temple construction moved speedily ahead. While Zerubbabel worked, the Lord watched with "these seven," that is, "the eyes of the LORD, which scan to and fro throughout the whole earth" (v. 10, cf. 3:9).

Nothing is hidden from God's infinite intelligence and omniscience. The Lord's eyes scrutinize the world. He providentially watches over and cares for Israel against its enemies and will accomplish His sovereign program for the Jewish people. God had commissioned the Temple's construction, and no one had a right to despise it.

Zechariah's message greatly encouraged both Zerubbabel and the Jewish remnant, both of whom were equipped and sustained by God's Spirit to finish building the second Temple. Zerubbabel completed the work four years later in 516 B.C. (Ezra 6:15).

Zechariah's Response

Excited about the revelation he had received and knowing that his question about the olive trees (Zech. 4:4) had not been answered, Zechariah quickly responded with one question and then another:

> What are these two olive trees—at the right of the lampstand and at its left? . . . What are these two olive branches [literally "ears of olives," "a cluster of olives"] that drip into the receptacles of the two gold pipes from which the golden oil drains? (vv. 11–12; cf. v. 3).

Again, the angel answered Zechariah's question with a question: "Do you not know what these are?"

Zechariah responded again, "No, my lord" (v. 13).

Then the angel revealed, "These are the two anointed ones, who stand beside the Lord of the whole earth" (v. 14). The word *these* refers to the two branches of the olive tree (v. 12) and, indirectly, to the two olive trees (v. 11). The two are "anointed sons" (literally "sons of oil"), or channels through which oil flows.

Anointing oil was used to consecrate high priests and kings; it was poured over their heads to symbolize their being endowed with God's Spirit.

Though not stated, Zerubbabel (the civil leader) and Joshua (the high priest) represent the two anointed ones who "stand by the Lord of the whole earth." Zerubbabel, a descendant of King David, and Joshua were anointed servants chosen by the Lord to head the nation and represent Israel before Him.

They also prefigure the two witnesses in Revelation 11:4 who are described as olive trees and lampstands, filled with the Holy Spirit as the witnesses of Christ during the Tribulation shortly before He returns to earth.

The lampstand, together with Zerubbabel and Joshua, prefigures Jesus the Messiah who will function as the Messianic King-Priest at His Second Coming. He will be the Light of a godly Temple in the Millennium, reign and rule as King-Priest, and bring blessing through a redeemed Israel as Lord and Light to the nations of the world.

The prophet's message is an encouragement to believers today. Everyone serving the Lord needs the anointing power of the Holy Spirit. His servants should never despise small beginnings when the Lord is in them. God is sovereign over the earth, and His prophetic program will succeed and accomplish what He has divinely decreed. Truly, it is neither by might, nor by power, but by the Spirit of God that a servant accomplishes the Lord's work.

CHAPTER 6

Israel's Wickedness Removed

Zechariah 5:1-11

Zechariah's first five visions greatly encouraged and comforted the Jewish remnant returning from Babylon. They revealed that the Lord would return to Jerusalem with mercy, give Israel victory over its enemies, reestablish and enlarge Jerusalem, purify and reinstate Israel's high priest, and assure completion of the Temple.

However, the last three visions in this series take an abrupt turn. Instead of foretelling blessing, they warned sternly against wickedness. Before Israel could experience the blessings, the land had to be purged from individual and national wickedness. Two of the last three visions are recorded in chapter 5 and address the issue of individual and national wickedness within the nation of Israel.

The Sixth Vision

The sixth vision was revealed to Zechariah as he contemplated his previous visions:

> Then I turned and raised my eyes, and saw there a flying scroll. And he said to me, "What do you see?" So I answered, "I see a flying scroll. Its length is twenty cubits and its width ten cubits" (Zech. 5:1–2).

What the prophet saw was a huge, unrolled scroll, 30 feet long and 15 feet wide, flying swiftly through the sky like a long banner, inscribed with God's Law on each side. Commentators compare the scroll's size to the holy place in the Tabernacle (Ex. 26:15–25) and the porch of Solomon's Temple (1 Ki. 6:3), but no comparison is alluded to in the text.

The angel told Zechariah what the flying scroll represented:

> This is the curse that goes out over the face of the whole earth: "Every thief shall be expelled," according to this side of the scroll; and, "Every perjurer shall be expelled," according

to that side of it (Zech. 5:3).

The "curse" was a message of judgment addressed to Israel and destined to fall on all who broke the commandments. Leviticus 26 and Deuteronomy 28 are often called the "blessing and cursing" chapters of the Mosaic Law. There Moses set forth the blessings the Israelites would experience by obeying God's commandments (Lev. 26:1–13; Dt. 28:1–14) and the curses that would befall them if they disobeyed (Lev. 26:14–46; Dt. 28:15–68).

In this context, God's curse will fall on "every thief" and "every perjurer" (Zech. 5:3). In other words, those who break the eighth commandment (Ex. 20:15) by stealing and the third commandment by swearing falsely in God's name (v. 7) will be "expelled" (Zech. 5:3), or rooted out and removed from Israel.

Notice that in the Ten Commandments, swearing falsely is a sin against God, mentioned in the middle of the first tablet of five commandments; and stealing is a sin against men, mentioned in the middle of the second tablet. The first is a sin against the holiness of God, and the second is a sin against one's neighbor. God probably chose these two commandments because they represented sins against both God and man.

Those who break God's Law will not be able to hide from His curse or escape His judgment. Zechariah continued,

> *"I will send out the curse," says the* LORD *of hosts; "it shall enter the house of the thief and the house of the one who swears falsely by My name. It shall remain [literally, "take up lodging"] in the midst of his house and consume it, with its timber and stones"* (v. 4).

God's curse moves throughout the households of Israel, looking to apprehend offenders. When an offender is found, he will be judged surely, swiftly, and severely. Even the offender's dwelling will be destroyed. The curse will spend the night in the house of the guilty party, consuming the materials the house was built with—the timber and stone. This metaphor is reminiscent of the fire sent down from heaven on the prophet Elijah's altar. It consumed the offering, wood, stones, dust, and water (1 Ki. 18:38).

The message in this sixth vision is that God will judge all persistent wickedness committed by the returning remnant. No Israelites will be able to conceal their sin or escape God's retribution. Sin will ruin the individuals and their families, especially those who steal and swear falsely. God's judgment will abide on both the house and family of all who commit wickedness until they are totally destroyed.

The Seventh Vision

In verse five, the interpreting angel instructed Zechariah to lift up his eyes and identify something. Unable to identify what he saw, Zechariah answered, "What is it?" (Zech. 5:6).

The angel replied,

> "It is a basket [ephah] that is going forth." He also said, "This is their resemblance [literally "eye" or "appearance"] throughout the earth: Here is a lead disc [talent] lifted up, and this is a woman sitting inside the basket"; then he said, "This is Wickedness!" And he thrust her down into the basket, and threw the lead cover over its mouth (vv. 6–8).

In the sixth vision, Zechariah learned God would permanently eradicate all wicked individuals from the land. Vision seven progressed further and pictured God permanently eradicating all wickedness from Israel.

The "basket" (Hebrew, *ephah*) mentioned in verse 6 was a large measuring container, slightly larger than a bushel, which could hold 10 omers (Ex. 16:36), or approximately five gallons of dry material. The text does not say what the basket represents, but many interpreters teach it symbolizes commercialism or trade carried on in Israel.

The Judeans were an agrarian people before their captivity in Babylon; but while they were in exile, say some interpreters, they learned commerce and became astute businessmen. The generation born in Babylon then picked up a spirit of secularism with a desire for material gain; and upon returning to the land, they brought these sinful practices with them. Scripture clearly shows that such practices were manifested among the returnees (Neh. 5:1–13; Mal. 3:8–9).

These interpreters believe the text further supports their position because it says, "This [the basket] is their [the Jewish people's] resemblance [eye or appearance] throughout the earth [or land]" (Zech. 5: 6). That is, the resemblance or eye represents the returnees' insatiable, self-centered look and desire for material gain through wicked practices learned in Babylon.

Such an interpretation reads into the text a depiction of the returnees that is not taught in vision seven. Thus it is best to interpret this vision as a general banishment of wickedness from Israel, rather than as a caricature of the returnees.

Next, the angel lifted the round covering from the basket to reveal a "woman sitting inside" (v. 7). She is identified as "Wickedness" (v. 8), that is, the personification of wickedness that was being manifested throughout the land of Israel.

Evidently, the woman tried to escape her confinement, but the angel "thrust her down [violently hurled her back] into the basket, and threw the lead cover over its mouth" (v. 8). The woman's incarceration limited her activities, preventing her from spreading further evil throughout Israel until she could finally be removed from the land.

The ultimate removal of wickedness in Israel and the world will take place before Christ's Millennial Reign. In that day, wickedness will not be manifested because Satan will be chained in the bottomless pit, unable to roam the earth and tempt men to do evil (Rev. 20:1–3); and Christ will rule Earth with a "rod of iron" (Ps. 2:8–9; Rev. 19:15).

Again, Zechariah looked up. This time he saw "two women, coming with the wind in their wings; for they had wings like the wings of a stork, and they lifted up the basket between earth and heaven" (Zech. 5:9). Storks have wings that are large, broad, strong, and able to carry the migratory birds for a long time over great distances without tiring. The word *stork* in Hebrew means "faithful one." The wind assisted the women as they swiftly and faithfully removed the basket of wickedness from the land of Israel and flew it to a chosen destination.

Some identify these women as Satan's demonic agents, seeking to remove the woman of wickedness from God's judgment in Israel. They fly the woman to Babylon and enshrine her there to be worshiped during the Great Tribulation.

Others identify the women as God's agents removing wickedness from Israel. There is no hint in the text as to the women's identity, but the second view seems more plausible. As the basket is lifted off the ground and flown away, Zechariah asks, "Where are they carrying the basket?" (v. 10).

The interpreting angel informed the prophet, "To build a house [abode] for it in the land of Shinar [Babylon]; when it is ready, the basket will be set there on its base" (v. 11). Wickedness is to be removed from Israel and returned to Babylon, where it originated. Some teach that, after the basket is firmly on its base, the woman inside is worshiped as an idol, but nothing in verse 11 leads to this conclusion or justifies this interpretation.

Shinar is where the cities of Babel, Erech, Accad, and Calneh were located (Gen. 10:10; 11:2). In Babel, under the guidance of Nimrod, the people said, "Come, let us build ourselves a city, and a tower whose top is in the heavens; let us make a name for ourselves, lest we be scattered abroad over the face of the whole earth" (11:4). This activity was in disobedience to God, who instructed Noah and his descendants after they left the ark to "fill the [whole] earth" (9:1).

In open rebellion to God's command, the people built a tower and placed a temple at its top. Their rebellion manifested itself in unity, strength, and pride as they developed a pagan religious system. In response, God confounded their language and scattered them around the world, which ended the construction on the city of Babel.

But the people did not cease their idolatry. They spread their religious practices across the earth, and the ungodly beliefs of many religions today can be traced to the idolatry of Babylon.

How will the wickedness mentioned throughout chapter 5 relate to Babylon in the future? Babylon is destined to rise from the ashes to play a major role in end-times events. The name Babylon brings to mind unsavory images of a wicked city-state with an abominable religious, political, and commercial system.

In the 1980s, Saddam Hussein started to rebuild portions of the ancient city of Babylon. Christians began to ask whether Hussein's project had anything to do with Bible prophecy, rekindling the often-asked question, "Did prophecy predict the rebuilding of Babylon?"

Conservative scholars differ on what the Bible teaches concerning Babylon's future. Some say the city will never be rebuilt for the following reasons:

> (1) Isaiah predicted, "Babylon . . . will be as when God overthrew Sodom and Gomorrah. It will never be inhabited, nor will it be settled from generation to generation; nor will the Arabian pitch tents there, nor will the shepherds make their sheepfolds there" (Isa. 13:19–20).

> (2) Jeremiah predicted no stone from Babylon's ruins

would be used to rebuild the city, and no one would dwell there (Jer. 51:26, 43).

(3) In Revelation 17—18, the word *Babylon* is a symbolic description of a wicked religious, political, and commercial system—not of a future, rebuilt city.

The reasons in favor of believing Babylon will be rebuilt during the Tribulation include the following:

(1) Babylon was not suddenly and completely destroyed, as were the cities of Sodom and Gomorrah; nor did it drink the last of God's wrath when captured by the Medo-Persian Empire in 539 B.C.

(2) The area is still inhabited, and stones from the old Babylon are being used to rebuild the city.

(3) Israel and Judah did not reunite, flee the city, come to the Lord in tears, or find rest from sorrow and fear (Isa. 14:3–4; Jer. 50:4–5, 8) when Babylon was destroyed.

These unfulfilled prophecies seem to indicate that Babylon will be rebuilt with a commercial system that will function on a worldwide scale and play a major role in end-time events.

In Revelation 17—18, John outlined the rise and fall of Babylon during the Tribulation. Events in these chapters represent an ecclesiastical, political, and commercial Babylonian system.

The apostle John described Babylon as a "great harlot" (Rev. 17:1). The word *harlot* (Greek, *porneia*) means "fornication," "adultery," or "prostitution" and refers to Babylon's abominable religious idolatry. Its perverted paganism will become the epitome of spiritual idolatry and will reach its peak during the first half of the Tribulation.

The harlot is pictured sitting on "many waters" (Rev. 17:1), later described as "peoples, multitudes, nations, and tongues" (v. 15). Captivated by Babylon's charm, the whole world will become intoxicated by its idolatrous religious system. "The kings of the earth committed fornication, and the inhabitants of the earth were made drunk with the wine of her fornication" (v. 2), wrote the apostle. Babylon will dominate the world by permeating every area of society: pagan religions, apostate Christianity, and political powers (cf. Rev. 14:8).

In Revelation 17:3, the harlot is sitting on a scarlet-colored beast, full of names of blasphemy, having seven heads and 10 horns. The Beast is the revived Roman Empire and, more specifically, its ruler (the Antichrist), who embodies the spirit of the Roman Empire (13:1). He will control the empire's political system. The seven heads are seven successive world empires of the past, leading up to the final unveiling of the revived Roman Empire. The 10 horns are 10 kings within the confederacy of the revived Roman Empire over whom the Beast will rule. The Beast is robed in scarlet, a color symbolic of luxury and splendor.

The harlot's depravity is seen in her unholy alliance with such a despicable political ruler. Church and state will be wed together as the woman rides the Beast (uses the political system to spread her false religious beliefs). In the first half of the Tribulation, each system will use the other to promote its ambition of world domination. At this point, the religious system will have a dominating influence over the political system.

The woman riding the Beast is arrayed in purple and scarlet, bedecked with gold and precious stones and pearls, and holds a golden cup (17:4). She is covered with gold from head to toe. Precious stones and pearls symbolize ostentatious extravagance. The gold cup she holds is full of abominations and the filthiness of her fornication. The word *abomination* expresses idolatrous worship and the immoral practices associated with it. In this passage, it expresses the woman's polluted character and practices. Those who partake of the harlot's poisonous cup of idolatry are destined to perish with her.

The woman has written on "her forehead . . . MYSTERY, BABYLON THE GREAT, THE MOTHER OF HARLOTS AND OF THE ABOMINATIONS OF THE EARTH" (v. 5). Scripture does not specify whether this identifying statement is in her flesh or on a headband like the ones worn by Roman prostitutes. The word *mystery* (Greek, *mysterion*) is not part of her title. In the New Testament, the word *mystery* refers to a revelation hidden in the past but revealed in the present.

An in-depth study of Revelation 17 may raise confusion about the exact meaning of the phrase *BABYLON THE GREAT*. In addition, various Bible scholars hold divergent interpretations. Most conservative scholars have embraced one of the following positions:

> (1) The word *Babylon* represents an ecclesiastical and political Babylon. "Ecclesiastical Babylon" refers to apostate Christendom (i.e., a one-world church including non-Christian religions) with headquarters in Rome (vv. 1–6). "Political Babylon" is a revival of the Roman Empire, the last form of Gentile world dominion, headed by the Beast (vv. 7–18).

> (2) The word *Babylon* refers to the religious and political systems mentioned above, as well as to a rebuilt city of Babylon near the Euphrates River.

> (3) Revelation 17 refers to the rebuilt city of Babylon whose end-times existence and subsequent annihilation were predicted by Isaiah, Jeremiah, and Zechariah. According to this interpretation, Babylon is a literal city of religious and political significance yet to be rebuilt. The text says, "The woman whom you saw is that great city which reigns over the kings of the earth" (v. 18).

It is clear from Revelation 17 that "MYSTERY, BABYLON" is linked to Rome religiously and politically, but it would seem from Revelation 18 that Babylon may be rebuilt.

The city's diabolical religious system can be traced from Nimrod's establishment of Babel (Gen. 10:8–10), later called Babylon. Nimrod built a huge tower, known as a ziggurat, of sun-dried bricks on the plains of Shinar (11:4). The tower was recognized as a temple or rallying center and a symbol of mankind's pride and rebellion against God. Other nations followed suit and constructed similar towers in honor of their heathen deities. God poured out judgment on this rebellious act by confounding the language and scattering the people across the face of the earth (vv. 7–9).

However, this fact did not spell the demise of the Babylonian religious system. History records that Nimrod's wife Semiramis became the head priestess of an idolatrous system of secret religious rituals known as Babylonian Mysteries. Babylon became the fountainhead of idolatry and the mother of every pagan system that spread across the world.

Semiramis supposedly gave birth to a son named Tammuz who was miraculously conceived by a sunbeam. He was presented to the people as a savior in fulfillment of the promise made to Eve concerning her seed (3:15). Tradition says Tammuz was killed by a wild boar; but after the people fasted for 40 days, he was resurrected from the dead on the feast of Ishtar. This legend of a mother-son cult became part of the Babylonian Mystery ritual and was quickly included in other idolatrous religious practices worldwide. The mother-son cult was headed by a priesthood that promoted salvation by means of (1) sprinkling of holy water, (2) ceremonial cleansing, and (3) purgatorial cleansing after death. Semiramis established an order of virgins dedicated to religious prostitution. She became known and worshiped as the "queen of heaven."

Ezekiel condemned the practice of Jewish "women weeping for Tammuz" (Ezek. 8:14). Jeremiah condemned Judah for offering cakes and burning incense to the "queen of heaven" (Jer. 7:18; 44:17–19, 25). Zechariah personified wickedness as a woman who will be reestablished in the land of Shinar (Babylon) in the latter days (Zech. 5:6–11).

After the Medo-Persian Empire captured Babylon, its city and temples were eventually destroyed. The Babylonian cult survived and found a new home in Pergamos of Asia Minor. It thrived under the name Etruscan Mysteries and eventually was headquartered in Rome. The chief priests wore miters shaped like the head of a fish in honor of Dagon the fish-god, considered the lord of life—another form of the Tammuz mystery.

In Rome, the chief priest took the title Pontifex Maximus. When Julius Caesar became head of the Roman Empire, he took the name Pontifex Maximus, a title held by all of the Roman emperors down to Constantine the Great, who became head of both church and state. The title was later adopted by the bishop of Rome. Over time, the church in Rome absorbed many of the Babylonian practices and idolatrous teachings, obscuring the true meaning of Scripture with such teachings as the worship of the virgin Mary and various festivals such as Easter, also known as Ishtar, one of the titles of the Babylonian "queen of heaven." Many of these teachings can be attributed to Constantine who combined paganism with Christianity when he adopted Christianity as a state religion.

Today a number of Protestant denominations have turned a blind eye to the antibiblical teachings found in Roman Catholicism, are cooperating in various religious functions with the Roman Church, and are even making overtures to reunite with it. Christendom will ultimately give birth to a one-world church after the Rapture of true believers.

John "saw the woman, drunk with the blood of the saints and with the blood of the martyrs of Jesus" (Rev. 17:6). This woman will not tolerate competition from other religious beliefs and will pour out her cruelties on the defenseless Tribulation saints. She will be drunk with human blood, which will inflame her insatiable lust for more violence as she attempts to destroy everything to do with Christ and His followers. The Antichrist will assist her by providing the necessary political power. This savage persecution will be against Tribulation believers, not the church, which will already have been raptured. Tribulation saints will be massacred on a worldwide scale (cf. 6:9–11; 7:14; 11:7; 13:7) for faithfully proclaiming their belief in Jesus.

Suddenly, the "ten horns" (Revived Roman Empire, Rev. 17:16) that follow the Beast will make an abrupt turnabout. They will awaken from their drunken stupor with the woman, whose charm and seduction will have lost their allure. Their love for her will turn to "hate" (v. 16); and then 10 kings, along with the Beast, will destroy her prior to the midpoint of the Tribulation.

They will make "her desolate" (v. 16), or divest her of all of the wealth she confiscated. They will make her "naked" (v. 16), stripping away her personal support, position, power, and prestige, thus exposing her moral corruption. They shall "eat her flesh" (v. 16) like the wild dogs that devoured the corpse of Jezebel (cf. 1 Ki. 21:23; 2 Ki. 9:30–37). They will "burn her with fire" (Rev. 17:16), eliminating all vestiges of her identity and her false religious system. Israel's law required that those who committed extreme acts of sin be burned with fire after their deaths to eradicate all memory of them (Lev. 20:14; 21:9; Josh. 7:15, 25).[1]

These hostile actions against the harlot will be initiated by God: "For God has put it into their hearts to fulfill His purpose" (Rev. 17:17)—that is, to rid the world of her pseudo-religious system. At times, Satan is allowed to manifest his will through nations to accomplish God's purposes, as in Revelation 16, when demons go out to gather all nations to Israel for the battle of Armageddon (vv. 13–14). The kings will believe they are carrying out their own program for conquest as they destroy the woman (harlot); but in actuality, they will accomplish God's purposes.

---

[1] Robert L. Thomas, *Revelation 8–22, An Exegetical Commentary* (Chicago: Moody Press, 1995), 304.

With the woman destroyed, the Antichrist will unite the world's religious and political systems under his control. The 10 nations will agree to "give their kingdom to the beast, until the words of God are fulfilled" (17:17). God's prophetic program will reach its intended goal as He sovereignly allows the kingdoms of this world to come under the Beast's control until the end of the Tribulation.[2] Then Earth's cup of wickedness will be full, and Christ will destroy the entire system on His Second Coming.

As we already mentioned, Revelation 18 makes it highly likely the city of Babylon will be rebuilt and play a major role in end-times events. Although Babylon's destruction is yet future, in God's eyes it is already accomplished. With a strong voice, an angel cries, "Babylon the great is fallen, is fallen, and has become a dwelling place of demons, a prison for every foul spirit, and a cage for every unclean and hated bird!" (v. 2). This once-thriving metropolis will become a wilderness stalked by imprisoned evil spirits that will hover over it like scavenger birds over their prey.

In part, the city's fall will be due to its decadent relationship with "all nations," described as "fornication" (v. 3). In the Tribulation, unbelievers, including kings and merchants, will be wooed into a wicked union with Babylon. They will become intoxicated with passion for its wealth. Political and corporate leaders "have become rich through the abundance of her luxury" (v. 3).

God will remember Babylon's spiritual and moral evil and judge the city accordingly. Its sins will have "reached to heaven" (v. 5). The word *reach* means to "glue" or "weld together"—that is, pile one on top of another, as bricks in a building. This is an allusion to the tower of Babel, which began ancient Babylon's wicked history (Gen. 11:3–9).[3] God will permit sin to increase until the cup is full; then He will act in divine judgment.

The angel calls for the law of retribution to be implemented against Babylon: "Repay her double according to her works; in the cup which she has mixed, mix double for her" (Rev. 18:6). Babylon's cup, used to seduce others, will be filled with God's undiluted wrath and used to destroy Babylon. No mercy will be shown. God will measure out twice as much judgment on the city because of the enormity of its sin.

The city will also fall due to its pride of wealth: "She glorified herself and lived luxuriously" (v. 7). The phrase "denotes a luxurious lifestyle with

---

[2] John F. Walvoord, *The Revelation of Jesus Christ* (Chicago: Moody Press, 1996), 257.
[3] Walvoord, 260.

the accompanying trappings of discourtesy, arrogance, self-indulgence, ruthless exercise of strength, and unruliness."[4]

Its self-glorification will lead to self-sufficiency, self-deification, and, finally, self-deception. Babylon will boast in its heart, "I sit as queen, and am no widow, and will not see sorrow" (v. 7; cf. Isa. 47:8–11). However, the opposite is true. It will be deceived and suffer all of the sorrow of widowhood.

Although the kings of the earth glorify it with praise, God will forsake the city. Its destruction will be sudden and complete. In "one day" it will suffer "death and mourning and famine. And she will be utterly burned with fire" (Rev. 18:8; cf. vv. 10, 17, 19). In 539 b.c., ancient Babylon was captured on the very night God prophesied its fall (Dan. 5).

A worldwide lament will rise from the Earth dwellers as they see the smoke of Babylon's destruction. Monarchs who committed fornication and lived luxuriously with Babylon will bewail its destruction (Rev. 18:9). Kings will wring their hands and weep over the power they once enjoyed by participating in Babylon's wickedness and wealth. They will mourn as if lamenting the passing of a loved one.

Merchants will mourn their tremendous loss as Babylon's lavish goods are destroyed (v. 11). The merchants will have exported not only their products worldwide but the diabolical Babylonian system as well, using sorceries (pseudo magical arts) to deceive the nations during the Tribulation and lure them into an immoral spiritual relationship with Babylon.

Now they will be bereft of their goods. All of the opulence and wealth mentioned in Revelation 18:12–13 will disappear in an hour, and access to the merchandise will be lost forever. The merchants will lament with "weeping and wailing" and great anguish (v. 15).

Even the mariners, every shipmaster and sailor, will grieve. They will heap dust on their heads as a sign of great mourning as they weep over their sudden loss (vv. 17–19).

In contrast to the monarchs, merchants, and mariners who lament Babylon's demise, heaven—along with the holy apostles and prophets—will rejoice over it. God, in His righteous judgment, will avenge the blood of the saints (18:20). He will recompense Babylon by afflicting it as it afflicted the saints who were martyred (cf. 6:9–11).

---

[4] Thomas, 325.

Babylon will go down like a great millstone cast into the sea: suddenly, swiftly, violently, and completely (cf. Jer. 51:61–64). The angel in Revelation 18 assures the world that Babylon will be found no more (Rev. 18:21). The word *anymore* (*no more*, KJV) appears seven times in this chapter. All sounds of life will cease to exist when God destroys the city. This will be a testimony to Babylon's total destruction, like that of Sodom and Gomorrah.

During the Tribulation, Babylon will be charged with murdering prophets and saints (v. 24; cf. Jer. 51:35–36, 49). Its aggressive hatred for true believers will be transmitted worldwide as it inspires governments to martyr them.

The sins of the Babylonian demonic system touch every major area of human existence:

- Politically, Babylon symbolizes prideful rebellion against God. By trying to build a tower to heaven, Nimrod attempted to confederate mankind into a city-state that would receive worldwide fame and recognition. He did so in direct defiance of God's command to "multiply, and fill the earth" (Gen. 9:1). God destroyed this program by confusing the language and scattering the inhabitants.

- Religiously, Babylon symbolizes the mother of idolatrous religion and worship that has infected all nations with its satanic dogma and practice.

- Economically, Babylon symbolizes the pride of wealth and sensuality; the worship of money, power, and prosperity; the spirit of covetous commercialism that dominates worldwide commerce.

Immediately prior to Christ's Second Coming, rebuilt Babylon, with its extensive commercial center, will be suddenly and swiftly destroyed (Rev. 18:2, 18, 21). Afterward, all wickedness will be removed from the earth in preparation for Christ's Millennial rule. What a day of glory that will be for both Israel and the world!

CHAPTER 7

Messiah's Coronation and Reign
Zechariah 6:1–15

What a long night Zechariah must have experienced. He had already received seven apocalyptic visions unveiling Israel's future, and the eighth was soon to come. This final vision would reveal God's judgment of the nations, symbolized by war chariots covering the earth.

After these visions, Joshua was crowned high priest. Although it was only a symbolic act, his crowning was meant as a type or foreshadowing of the Messiah, who will be crowned both Priest and King at His return.

The revelation in chapter 6 is a fitting culmination to the night visions and outlines prophetic events the Messiah will perform, events described more fully here.

The Chariots of Judgment

Zechariah unveiled his eighth vision from God: "Then I turned and raised my eyes and looked, and behold, four chariots were coming from between two mountains, and the mountains were mountains of bronze" (Zech. 6:1).

The first and eighth visions are similar, but differences do exist. In vision one, horsemen are on a reconnaissance patrol to evaluate the Gentile world that is living in peace; in vision eight, horse-drawn chariots arrive to implement judgment. In both visions, the horses are similar, yet different in color. In vision one, the horses stand in a ravine among the myrtle trees; in vision eight, they emerge from between two mountains made of bronze.

Although the bronze mountains are often considered to be Mount Zion and the Mount of Olives, the text is silent on their actual identity. Obviously, they are to be interpreted symbolically. In Scripture, bronze symbolizes God's divine righteousness and judgment. For example, the bronze serpent held up in the wilderness related to the judgment of sin (Num. 21:9). The description of Messiah's feet as being "like fine brass [bronze]" (Rev. 1:15) speaks of His judicial character in judging His enemies.

In Zechariah 6:2–3, the four horse-drawn chariots that come from between these two bronze mountains symbolize God's universal judgment. The colors of these horses are not explained in Zechariah, but Revelation 6:1–8 sheds light on the significance of the colored horses: Red symbolizes war; black, famine and death; and white, conquest and victory. There is no "dappled" horse (Zech. 6:3) in Revelation 6, but in Zechariah it may represent plagues and pestilence poured out on the earth. The black horses travel north, the white horses follow, and the dappled horses go south. Zechariah did not comment on the direction of the red horses.

Zechariah asked, "What are these, my lord?" (Zech. 6:4). The angel revealed these horses represent "four spirits [winds] of heaven, who go out from their station before the Lord of all the earth" (v. 5). These are angelic beings from heaven, ministers of God assigned to implement judgment on the rebellious nations of the world prior to Christ's return.

The strong horses were straining at the bit, "eager to go" (v. 7) and patrol the earth. The angel, speaking for God the Father, gave the order, "Go, walk to and fro throughout the earth" (v. 7), in readiness to implement judgment. Note that the mission is orchestrated by God Himself.

The Lord called to Zechariah, "Those who go toward the north country have given rest to My Spirit in the north country" (v. 8). That is, they appeased God's wrath by executing His judgment on the nations. This prophecy anticipates the future Day of the Lord's judgment in the Great Tribulation when God will destroy the evil system of Babylon and all of Israel's enemies (cf. 5:5–11; Rev. 17—18). Only then will God's Spirit be appeased and have complete rest.

The Crowning of Joshua

After the night visions, Zechariah received further instruction:

> Then the word of the LORD came to me, saying: "Receive the gift from the captives—from Heldai, Tobijah, and Jedaiah, who have come from Babylon—and go the same day and enter the house of Josiah the son of Zephaniah" (Zech. 6:9–10).

The text does not reveal when the instruction was given to Zechariah, but it must have been soon after the eighth vision.

The gift bearers were former Jewish captives from Babylon who did not return to Jerusalem under Zerubbabel (537 B.C.), Ezra (458 B.C.), or Nehemiah (445 B.C.). The Jewish delegation brought an offering of gold and silver to the Lord for the restoration of the second Temple.

Zechariah was to fashion an "elaborate crown" from the silver and gold and "set it on the head of Joshua the son of Jehozadak, the high priest" (v. 11). The word *crown* in Hebrew is plural and should be translated "crowns."

Some teach the crown possessed several circlets that formed a single crown. Others believe the term refers to a second crown made for Zerubbabel. However, a crown for Zerubbabel was out of the question because he was not a priest or a king but only a governor. To crown Zerubbabel the king of Israel would have been a premature attempt to restore the Davidic kingdom. No king in Israel's history was ever allowed to serve as both king and priest. That role is reserved for the Messiah alone. When King Uzziah entered the Temple in a priestly role, he was severely judged by God and became a leper until his death (2 Chr. 26:16–21).

I believe this is a double-ringed crown, symbolic of the priestly and kingly diadem the Messiah will wear at His coronation. Thus Joshua's crowning was a type or foreshadowing of the Messiah's crowning as both Priest and King. What a fitting conclusion to the eighth vision in Zechariah.

The crown placed on Joshua's head would be housed in the Temple for a memorial: "Now the elaborate crown shall be for a memorial in the temple of the LORD for Helem, Tobijah, Jedaiah, and Hen [*hen* means "graciousness" and is a nickname for Josiah] the son of Zephaniah" (Zech. 6:14). The ceremonial crown was to be kept in the Temple as a reminder of the Jewish delegation from Babylon that brought the gift to Jerusalem for the restoration of the Temple. It would also remind Israel of the teaching that one day Messiah will appear and be crowned the King-Priest of Israel.

Abruptly, Zechariah is commanded to deliver a message to Joshua: "Then speak to him [Joshua], saying, 'Thus says the LORD of hosts, saying: "Behold, the Man whose name is the BRANCH!"'" (Zech. 6:12). The word *Branch* is a Messianic title used four times in the Old Testament.

A number of prophecies are given concerning the Messianic Branch.

First, Messiah the Branch "shall branch out" (v. 12). Although He came at the First Advent as "a tender plant, and as a root out of dry ground" (Isa. 53:2), the Messiah would shoot upward and branch out as a strong, fast-growing plant elevated to great heights.

Second, Messiah the Branch "shall build the temple of the LORD" (Zech. 6:12). This verse does not refer to the second Temple that Zerubbabel constructed in 516 B.C. but to the Millennial Temple that will be constructed at Messiah's Second Coming (Isa. 2:2–4; Ezek. 40—42; Hag. 2:7–9).

Third, Messiah the Branch is to "bear [carry] the glory" (Zech. 6:13). The word *glory* refers to the majesty and splendor of God (Ps. 96:6). In the Millennial Kingdom, the Messiah will finally receive the honor, majesty, and glory due Him and reign with regal splendor as both King and Priest.

Fourth, Messiah the Branch "shall sit and rule on His throne" in the city of Jerusalem (Zech. 6:13). Having dispossessed Satan and his demons from their control of Earth, the Messiah will reclaim the planet as its Creator-Redeemer, sit on the throne of His father David (Lk. 1:32), and rule in righteousness with a rod of iron.

Fifth, Messiah the Branch will "be a priest on His throne, and the counsel of peace shall be between them both" (Zech. 6:13). The Messiah will exercise not only His Kingly role but His Priestly role as well. He is not a Priest from the Levitical, Aaronic priesthood but after the order of Melchizedek, king of Salem, who was both a king and priest (Ps. 110:4; Heb. 7).

Today Jesus the Messiah is seated at the right hand of God the Father, exercising only His Priestly role (Heb. 8:1–2). Tension and rivalry existed between Israel's king and priest throughout the nation's history. But in the Millennium, both offices will reside in Messiah the Branch who will function as a King-Priest, reconciling both positions and bringing peace to the world (Isa. 9:6; 11:1–2; 66:12).

Sixth, Messiah the Branch will build the Temple with gifts donated by righteous Gentiles: "Even those from afar shall come and build the temple of the LORD. Then you shall know that the LORD of hosts has sent Me to you" (Zech. 6:15). In other words, like the Jewish delegation from Babylon, Gentiles will bring gifts to Jerusalem; and the Messiah will use them to construct the Millennial Temple (Isa. 2:2–3; 60:5, 9, 11; 61:6). When the nations bring their wealth to Jerusalem, the entire world will know that God the Father sent the Messiah to Israel to build the Millennial Temple.

Seventh, Zechariah stated, "And this shall come to pass if you diligently obey the voice of the LORD your God" (Zech. 6:15). This phrase was first uttered by Moses in Deuteronomy 28:1 when God promised to bless Israel if the nation obeyed His commandments once it entered the land of Canaan. At first glance, God's promise to Israel in Zechariah 6:15 seems conditional and based on obedience to the Lord. However, such is not the case; the Messiah's rule and the Temple's construction are settled in God's sovereign plan. Zechariah was saying that an individual's participation in the Millennial Kingdom blessings will depend on that person's obedience to the Lord.

What is said about the Branch corresponds to what is presented about Christ in the four Gospels of the New Testament.

> *The Branch as Royal King*. "I will raise to David a Branch of righteousness; a King shall reign and prosper, and execute judgment and righteousness in the earth" (Jer. 23:5). This description corresponds to the Messiah's presentation as a righteous King in Matthew.

> *The Branch as Servant* (Zech. 3:8). Messiah is clearly identified as the Servant of the Lord, who came to do the Father's will by redeeming humanity (Isa. 42:1; 49:3–4; 50:10; 52:13; 53:11). This description corresponds to Messiah as a servant in Mark 10:45.

> *The Branch as Fully Man*. "The Man whose name is the BRANCH" (Zech. 6:12) corresponds to the presentation of the Messiah in Luke.

> *The Branch as Fully God*. "The Branch of the LORD" (Isa. 4:2) corresponds to the Messiah as the Son of God in John.[1]

These eight prophetic visions provided an overview of God's plan for Israel, keeping hope alive within the nation that one day its Messiah would come, be crowned both King and Priest, and fulfill all the prophecies described in these first six chapters.

---

[1] Walter C. Kaiser Jr., *The Preacher's Commentary: Micah–Malachi* (Nashville, TN: Thomas Nelson Publishers, 1992), 23:335.

CHAPTER 8

Fasting Without Fidelity

Zechariah 7:1–14

A delegation from Bethel arrived in Jerusalem to seek counsel from priests and prophets concerning fasting. They asked whether the annual fast commemorating the destruction of Solomon's Temple should be continued, since a rebuilt Temple was well on its way toward completion. Apparently, people were growing weary of keeping this fast, along with others they had instituted while exiled in Babylon. These fasts had become burdensome rituals devoid of spiritual significance.

In chapters 7 and 8, God addresses the delegation's question on fasting. Zechariah presented His answer in four messages that told the Bethel delegation what it needed to hear, not what it expected to hear. Each message was introduced with a form of the phrase *the word of the LORD of hosts came to me, saying* (7:4, 8; 8:1, 18).

Request by the People

Zechariah provided the date when he received the four messages from God: "Now in the fourth year of King Darius it came to pass that the word of the LORD came to Zechariah, on the fourth day of the ninth month, Chislev" (7:1). The prophet received this revelation on December 7, 518 B.C., 22 months after receiving the eight night visions (1:7).

Zechariah further stated that it was "when the people sent Sherezer, with Regem-Melech and his men, to the house of God, to pray before the LORD" (7:2). A better translation of the Hebrew is, "Now the town of Bethel had sent Sherezer and Regem-Melech and their men to seek the favor of the LORD." Instead of taking the Hebrew word *bethel* to mean the town by that name, both the King James and New King James versions recorded its literal meaning ("house of God"). However, the phrase *house of God* does not refer to the Temple under construction at the time of Zechariah's prophecy. The proper translation is "Bethel," referring to the city 12 miles north of Jerusalem, an ancient capital of the northern kingdom and the seat of idolatrous worship before it fell to the Assyrians in 722 B.C.

Sherezer and Regem-Melech are Babylonian names, indicating these two men were born during Judah's exile in Babylon. Many Jewish people, including the prophet Daniel, received Babylonian names while in exile. These men probably joined the returnees from Babylon to rebuild the city of Bethel (Ezra 2:28).

The delegation came to inquire of the priest and prophets: "Should I weep in the fifth month and fast as I have done for so many years?" (Zech. 7:3), referring to weeping over the destruction of Solomon's Temple after the Babylonians destroyed it on the ninth of Av in 586 B.C. (2 Ki. 25:8). This was a self-imposed fast not ordained by God. The Jewish people developed it during their captivity in Babylon to remember the destruction of Jerusalem and Solomon's Temple.

Over time, they developed mourning practices for the ninth of Av (*Tisha B'Av*) to deny themselves comfort and pleasure by refraining from using perfume and cosmetics, wearing leather shoes, bathing, shaving, and cutting hair. And they sat on low stools as a sign of mourning. It was customary to read Lamentations, Jeremiah, and parts of the Talmud that refer to the Temple's destruction and the laws of mourning.

The Israelites also established other fasts in relation to the Babylonian invasion. (See Zechariah 8:19.) The fourth-month fast was in memory of the destruction of the city's walls (Jer. 39:2), the seventh-month fast memorialized Gedaliah's assassination (2 Ki. 25:22–26), and the tenth-month fast was in memory of the Babylonian invasion (vv. 1–2).

The phrase *as I have done for so many years* (Zech. 7:3) seems to reveal that the delegation's true desire was to discontinue the self-imposed ceremony of fasting and mourning over the destruction of the Temple. Since the Temple was being rebuilt, they probably felt it unnecessary. Zechariah did not answer their question until he gave his fourth message (8:18–19).

Rebuke From the Prophet

In his first message, Zechariah launched into the motive of fasting with the words, *Then the word of the LORD of hosts came to me, saying* (7:4). The Lord's message through Zechariah was addressed to "all the people . . . and to the priests" (v. 5).

God asked two rhetorical questions about fasting. The first was, "When you fasted and mourned in the fifth and seventh months during those seventy years, did you really fast for Me—for Me?" (v. 5).

Thus Zechariah asked the people whether they fasted out of a dead, formal ritualism or from a heartfelt commitment. The question implies their fasting was selfish and not God-honoring. If such fasting does not honor God, it is merely external formalism and a total waste of time and effort.

Isaiah the prophet dealt with Israel's fasting as well. The Jewish people had fasted, but God did not respond to their request by giving them what they wanted. So they asked God, "Why have we fasted . . . and You have not seen? Why have we afflicted our souls, and You take no notice?" (Isa. 58:3). In other words, "God, why are we going to all this effort if what we are doing You do not notice? All our fasting is to no avail." Isaiah presented God's reply to Judah, which He had given in an earlier day:

> *Indeed you fast for strife and debate, and to strike with the fist of wickedness. You will not fast as you do this day, to make your voice heard on high. Is it a fast that I have chosen, a day for a man to afflict his soul? Is it to bow down his head like a bulrush, and to spread out sackcloth and ashes? Would you call this a fast, and an acceptable day to the LORD?*
>
> *Is this not the fast that I have chosen: to loose the bonds of wickedness, to undo the heavy burdens, to let the oppressed go free, and that you break every yoke? Is it not to share your bread with the hungry, and that you bring to your house the poor who are cast out; when you see the naked, that you cover him, and not hide yourself from your own flesh? Then your light shall break forth like the morning, your healing shall spring forth speedily, and your righteousness shall go before you; the glory of the LORD shall be your rear guard. Then shall you call, and the LORD will answer; you shall cry, and He will say, "Here I am." If you take away the yoke from your midst, the pointing of the finger, and speaking wickedness, if you extend your soul to the hungry and satisfy the afflicted soul, then your light shall dawn in the darkness, and your darkness shall be as the noonday. The LORD will guide you continually, and satisfy your soul in drought, and*

strengthen your bones; you shall be like a watered garden, and like a spring of water, whose waters do not fail. Those from among you shall build the old waste places; you shall raise up the foundations of many generations; and you shall be called the Repairer of the Breach, the Restorer of Streets to Dwell In.

If you turn away your foot from the Sabbath, from doing your pleasure on My holy day, and call the Sabbath a delight, the holy day of the LORD honorable, and shall honor Him, not doing your own ways, nor finding your own pleasure, nor speaking your own words, then you shall delight yourself in the LORD; and I will cause you to ride on the high hills of the earth, and feed you with the heritage of Jacob your father. The mouth of the LORD has spoken (Isa. 58:4–14).

The second rhetorical question brings out the true motive of their fasting: "When you eat and when you drink, do you not eat and drink for yourselves?" (Zech. 7:6). In other words, they fasted and feasted for a feeling of self-satisfaction. It was outward, ritualistic show that was empty of spiritual reality; God had no part in it.

Zechariah continued by asking his own question: "Should you not have obeyed the words which the LORD proclaimed through the former prophets when Jerusalem and the cities around it were inhabited and prosperous, and the South and the Lowland were inhabited?" (v. 7). The Israelites had received numerous warnings to obey God's Word wholeheartedly during times of prosperity in the land. All of their religious observances, such as fasting, were of no value, no matter how well executed, if not done from the heart in obedience to God's Word.

Warnings from the earlier prophets went unheeded during Israel's time of peace and prosperity. Judah did not listen then, but should it not listen now to God's warning? If these returning exiles ignored God's Word from Zechariah, they would be in great danger of provoking divine discipline as their forefathers had done. And if they exercised obedience to God's Word, they, too, could enjoy the peace and prosperity their forefathers had seen. They stood at a crossroads.

Remembering the Past

In his second message, Zechariah urged the returnees to remember that abuse in the area of social and personal relationships had brought divine discipline on both the land and their forefathers. Again, the Lord reiterated the age-old commandments that the Jewish people were obligated to keep toward one another:

> *Then the word of the LORD came to Zechariah, saying, "Thus says the LORD of hosts: 'Execute true justice, show mercy and compassion everyone to his brother. Do not oppress the widow or the fatherless, the alien or the poor. Let none of you plan evil in his heart against his brother'"* (vv. 8–10).

The Lord told Israel that duty to one's neighbor indicates a spiritual commitment to Him. He requires that justice be administered without partiality or bias. "Mercy [loving kindness] and compassion [love, pity, and concern for hurting people]" must be shown. One must not take advantage of widows, orphans, strangers, or the poor. In fact, the prophets continually exhorted the Israelites concerning their responsibility to love and care for these people.

Furthermore, the Law forbids plotting or imagining evil, revenge, or injury against another Israelite; these actions actually constitute the first step downward to domestic, business, and religious evil. Those who practiced such things lacked a spiritual relationship with God and were in danger of bringing judgment on themselves as did their preexilic forefathers.

Zechariah listed the ways their forefathers had responded to the messages of the preexilic prophets:

> *But they refused to heed, shrugged their shoulders, and stopped their ears so that they could not hear. Yes, they made their hearts like flint, refusing to hear the law and the words which the LORD of hosts had sent by His Spirit through the former prophets. Thus great wrath came from the LORD of hosts* (vv. 11–12).

Zechariah said their forefathers resisted and pulled away their shoulders (a sign of rejection) from submitting to God's ways as an ox turns its neck away from being yoked. They also plugged their ears to God's prophet. Refusing to listen to his message, they resisted his warning and held it in contempt. They made their hearts like "adamant stone," meaning their hearts were impervious to God's Word (Ezek. 3:7–9). This attitude caused God to pour His wrath out on Judah and yoke the survivors to the cruel nation of Babylon for 70 years of slavery.

Retribution Proclaimed

Zechariah addressed his second message to the Bethel delegation, recounting what the Lord did to their preexilic forefathers:

> *"Therefore it happened, that just as He proclaimed and they would not hear, so they called out and I would not listen," says the* LORD *of hosts. "But I scattered them with a whirlwind among all the nations which they had not known. Thus the land became desolate after them, so that no one passed through or returned; for they made the pleasant land desolate"* (Zech. 7:13–14).

Israel's disobedience to God brought His retribution on Israel. First, God turned a deaf ear to the Israelites' crying prayer for help. They refused to hear the prophet's message, so He acted in kind by choosing not to hear them.

Second, God dispersed their forefathers among the nations. The Lord scattered them like a tornado or hurricane swiftly removes everything its whirlwind touches (Lev. 26:14–43; Dt. 28:15–68). Israel was scattered "among all the nations which they had not known" (Zech. 7:14): Assyria (722 B.C.), Babylon (586 B.C.), Rome (A.D. 70), and then the world.

Third, the land of Israel was made desolate. Once called the "pleasant land" (literally, "land of desire, delight," v. 14) and "a land flowing with milk and honey" (Ex. 3:8), it now lay in ruins.

Whenever the Jewish people were dispossessed from their land, it became desolate and undeveloped. The only time the land blooms is when the Jewish people are in it. The past 1,900 years have shown this to be the case. With the return of the Jewish people in the 20th century, Israel has come alive and continues to be a modern, thriving country.

The Bethel delegation, along with all of Israel, was called to heed Zechariah's warning so that the nation would not repeat the error of its forefathers.

On the final page of the Old Testament (2 Chronicles is the last book in the Hebrew canon), we read, "But they mocked the messengers of God, despised His words, and scoffed at His prophets, until the wrath of the LORD arose against His people, till there was no remedy" (2 Chr. 36:16).

Is there not a message for our generation in these words? We, too, must listen to God's Word; or the same judgment will befall us.

CHAPTER 9

Israel's Glorious Restoration

Zechariah 8:1–23

In the previous chapter, a delegation from Bethel questioned the necessity of continuing to fast over the destruction of Solomon's Temple. Zechariah did not address the issue directly; instead, he used the question to reflect on how God disciplined the nation's forefathers in the past because of their disobedience (Zech. 7:8–14). He warned the returning remnant that their failure to repent of sin would bring the same judgment down on them (1:1–6).

In chapter 8, Zechariah turned from God's past discipline to bring the remnant a new message of hope. He focused on the Millennial Kingdom when Israel will experience restoration, renewal, peace, and prosperity. In that day, Israel's fasting will be replaced with joyful feasting. The phrase *the LORD of hosts* (used 18 times in this chapter) reassured Israel that God will fulfill His Kingdom promises.

Israel Restored

Zechariah began his third message to the delegation with the following statement:

> *Again the word of the LORD of hosts came, saying, "Thus says the LORD of hosts: 'I am zealous for Zion with great zeal; with great fervor I am zealous for her'"* (8:1–2).

In these opening verses, God clearly and repeatedly expressed His great love for Israel. The word *zealous* in Hebrew is the word for "jealous" and is used three times to express the depth and intensity of God's burning and passionate love for Israel. His love for the Jewish people will tolerate no rivals (Ex. 34:14) in much the same way that a husband claims exclusivity over his wife. God, in His righteous jealousy, comes to Israel's defense and wages war in great wrath against all who try to thwart His purposes and plans for this nation (Zech. 1:14–15; cf. Ezek. 38:18–19).

The Lord further stated, "I will return to Zion, and dwell in the midst of Jerusalem" (Zech. 8:3). This return and dwelling will take place at His Second Advent. In that day, the Lord will "dwell," or settle down, in Jerusalem and make the city His spiritual and political capital from which He will rule the world. Jerusalem will be called the "City of Truth" (v. 3) because the Messiah will rule in truth (Rev. 19:11). Zechariah 8:3 also states that the Temple Mount will be called "The Holy Mountain" because the Messiah's presence will sanctify it as the holy place where God will be worshiped in truth.

Jerusalem will become a city of peace, safety, security, and divine blessing where men and women, well advanced in age (Isa. 65:20), sit without fear for their safety. Boys and girls will also fill the streets of Jerusalem and laugh and play without fear (Zech. 8:4–5).

These promises might have seemed unbelievable to the Jewish people returning from exile in Babylon—or, for that matter, to any generation of Jewish people. So the Lord posed a rhetorical question:

> Thus says the LORD of hosts: "If it is marvelous [difficult] in the eyes of the remnant of this people in these [those] days, will it also be marvelous [difficult] in My eyes?" says the LORD of hosts (v. 6).

In other words, nothing is difficult or insurmountable for God, including delivering the Jewish people of Zechariah's generation— or any generation, for that matter. In fact, God will execute one of the greatest deliverances and gatherings of Jewish people at the end of the Great Tribulation (Isa. 11:11–12; 43:5–6; Mt. 24:31). In that day, Israel's relationship with the Lord will be restored, and God will again call the Jewish people "My people" (Zech. 8:7–8; 13:9; cf. Hos. 2:23). Notice the rhetorical question in verse 6 is bracketed with the words *says the LORD of hosts*, giving divine authority and assurance that Israel's deliverance at any time is never difficult for God.

Israel Renewed

The Lord then encouraged the remnant that had started to rebuild the Temple to finish the task:

> Thus says the LORD of hosts: "Let your hands be strong, you who have been hearing in these days these words by the mouth of the prophets, who spoke in the day the foundation

was laid for the house of the LORD of hosts, that the temple
might be built" (Zech. 8:9).

The prophets' names are not given, but most likely they were Haggai
and Zechariah. "Let your hands be strong" is meant to strengthen and
encourage Israel. Scripture gives two reasons why the Temple was not
built: "There were no wages for man nor any hire for beast; there was
no peace from the enemy for whoever went out or came in; for I set all
men, everyone, against his neighbor" (v. 10). First, the returning remnant
was poor and unable to afford the necessary resources to reconstruct the
Temple. Second, civil and political strife existed within and without the
Jewish community, hampering the work (Ezra 4:1–5; 5:3; 6:6, 13).

But that was then. Zechariah now had an encouraging word from the
Lord:

"But now I will not treat the remnant of this people as in the
former days," says the LORD of hosts (Zech. 8:11).

A new day had dawned. In the past, God had disciplined a disobedient
Israel, but now the nation would experience His favor and blessing.
Israel's land shall prosper: "For the seed shall be prosperous [literally,
"seed of peace"], the vine shall give its fruit, the ground shall give her
increase, . . . I will cause the remnant of this people to possess all these"
(v. 12).

The nation will sow its seed in a time of peace, and nothing will destroy
it. God will restore a heavy dew to the land (v. 12), causing the vine and
the ground to produce abundant fruit. This promise to the remnant will
find its greater fulfillment during the Millennial Kingdom (Amos 9:13–
15).

The Lord said to Israel, "Just as you were a curse among the
nations, . . . so I will save you, and you shall be a blessing" (Zech. 8:13). This
is the theme of chapter 8. In the past, Israel was cursed because it broke
God's commandments and practiced idolatry (Dt. 28:15–68). However,
the day will come when God will reverse the curse, "save" ("deliver," Zech.
8:13) Israel physically and spiritually, and make it a blessing among the
nations (Gen. 12:3).

Such a glorious promise was meant to calm and comfort Israel in
its hardship and give the nation courage to face the future. Therefore,
Zechariah commanded Israel, "Do not fear, let your hands be strong"
(Zech. 8:13). In other words, because of His purpose and plan for His

people, God commanded the Israelites to be diligent in their efforts, trusting the outcome to God.[1]

The Lord continued to provide Israel with assurance that His blessings will come to fruition:

> *"Just as I determined to punish you when your fathers provoked Me to wrath," says the LORD of hosts, "and I would not relent [repent or change His mind], so again in these days I am determined to do good to Jerusalem and to the house of Judah"* (vv. 14–15).

As it was in God's divine purpose to destroy Israel's forefathers because of their disobedience, so, too, is it in His plan to bless Jerusalem and Israel. This promise awaits future fulfillment.

In light of these promises, Israel was called to be spiritually and morally obedient to the Lord and was commanded to practice four things that would provide evidence of a restored relationship with God. First, Israel was to "speak each man the truth to his neighbor" (v. 16). Speaking truth would prove the relationship with God had been restored. Second, Israel was to "give judgment in [its] gates for truth, justice, and peace" (v. 16). Court decisions administered in truth at the city gate would show that justice prevailed throughout Israel and bring peace to the nation. Third, "Let none of you think evil in your heart against your neighbor" (v. 17); that is, do not plan wickedness in your mind against a fellow Israelite. Fourth, "do not love a false oath" (v. 17); do not commit perjury in a court of law against your neighbor. God hates all of these sins (v. 17; cf. Prov. 6:16–19).

Israel to Rejoice

Zechariah waited to answer the delegates' question about fasting until his fourth and final message. With the return of the remnant, a new age had dawned, and all of their fasting (the fourth-, fifth-, seventh-, and tenth-month fasts) would become "cheerful feasts" (Zech. 8:19) because of the blessing Israel would experience through its restoration and spiritual renewal.

This joy is a foretaste of what Israel and the world will experience in a fuller way during the Messiah's Millennial Reign. Because of future

---

[1] J. Carl Laney, *Zechariah* (Chicago, IL: Moody Press, 1984), 88.

blessings through God's grace and faithfulness, Israel is admonished to "love truth and peace" (v. 19).

Israel's restoration and spiritual renewal will bring blessing to the entire world. Gentiles from "many cities" will urge one another to make a pilgrimage to Jerusalem to worship the Lord and seek His favor; the response is, "I myself will go also" (v. 21). The prophet emphasized the certainty of this prophecy: "Yes, many peoples and strong nations shall come to seek the LORD of hosts in Jerusalem and to pray before the LORD" (v. 22).

Messiah's rule in Jerusalem will be the main attraction for the nations coming to Israel. During the Millennium, redeemed Gentiles who come to Jerusalem will want to learn from the Jewish people: "In those days ten men from every language of the nations shall grasp the sleeve of a Jewish man, saying, 'Let us go with you, for we have heard that God is with you'" (v. 23). Immediately on arriving in the city, 10 men will seize the corner of a passing Jewish man's garment with such intensity that they will not let go.

What nations have sought through humanistic endeavor, redeemed mankind will realize in the God of Israel. Jewish men will be priests and ministers of God, teaching the nations what they need to know concerning the Lord in Jerusalem (Isa. 61:6). This is the day when God's promise to the nations, "In you [Israel] all the families of the earth shall be blessed" (Gen. 12:3), comes to full fruition. In that day, the nations and Israel will rejoice in the Lord's reign and their redemption.

CHAPTER 10

The Grecian Conqueror
Zechariah 9:1–8

The six remaining chapters of Zechariah's prophecy consist of events pertaining to God's eschatological program for Israel. They cover a vast period that extends from the Grecian era under Alexander the Great to the yet-future return of Israel's Messiah. Some of the clearest, most abundant Messianic prophecies on the Lord's First and Second Advents are revealed in Zechariah 9—14.

These six chapters separate into two divisions with the phrase *the burden of the word of the LORD* (9:1; 12:1). The first burden (oracle) reiterates Alexander's historical conquest of the East and the appearing of Israel's Messianic Shepherd (9:1—11:17). The second describes events surrounding Messiah's Second Coming and His Kingdom rule as they relate to Israel's restoration and redemption (12:1—14:21).

Theologians disagree on when Zechariah 9:1–8 was fulfilled. We will not compare views here. Most conservative scholars teach the passage took place during the time of Alexander the Great.

Judgment Declared

God's judgment of the nations surrounding Israel was inevitable:

The burden [oracle] of the word of the LORD against the land of Hadrach, and Damascus its resting place (For the eyes of men and all the tribes of Israel are on the LORD); also against Hamath, which *borders on it, and against Tyre and Sidon, though they are very wise* (vv. 1–2).

The word *burden* means "to lift up" or "to bear" and refers to something heavy and burdensome, such as this indictment from the Lord. Zechariah had to deliver the ominous message that God would pour out judgment on Israel's neighbors.

To do so, God would use Alexander the Great. Daniel had prophesied earlier that the Grecian Empire, like a winged leopard (Dan. 7:6) and strong male goat (8:5–7), would swiftly conquer Asia. With his army of 40,000, Alexander rapidly defeated the Persians at the Battle of Issus in 333 B.C. King Darius escaped. But rather than pursue him, Alexander focused on attacking Phoenicia and Egypt.

Zechariah mentioned cities Alexander conquered on his way to Egypt. Hadrach (Zech. 9:1) appears only here in Scripture. Scholars have interpreted the word in various ways: (1) symbolically and mystically; (2) as the name of an Assyrian king or fire-god; (3) as the name of a deity in Eastern Aramea; and (4) as a scribal error for Hauran, a district south of Damascus connected with Hamath. We may safely identify Hadrach with Hatarikka, a city north of Hamath, mentioned in an Assyrian inscription as the opponent of Tiglath-Pileser III who conquered it in 738 B.C.

Damascus (v. 1) was the capital of Aram (Syria), a strong enemy of Israel for many centuries. God's wrath will "rest," or settle, on Damascus first.

Hamath (v. 2) was an Aramean (Syrian) city north of Damascus on the Orontes River. Tyre and Sidon (v. 2) were ancient Phoenician cities on the coastal plain, with the mountains of Lebanon on the east and the Mediterranean Sea on the west. All of these nations, including Israel, had their "eyes . . . on the LORD" (v. 1), meaning they stood in awe at God's judgment through Alexander the Great.

Verses 3 and 4 describe Tyre's destruction. Tyre was an impregnable fortress that had grown rich through commerce. Silver there was as common as dust; and gold, as common as dirt—making the city self-sufficient (cf. Ezek. 28:4–5). Nevertheless, Tyre would not survive: "The LORD will cast her out; He will destroy her power in the sea" (Zech. 9:4).

Nebuchadnezzar besieged Tyre from 586–573 B.C. and eventually destroyed it. But many of the inhabitants escaped to a fortified island. Alexander scraped up the ruins of old Tyre and dumped the debris into the sea, enabling him to build a half-mile causeway so that his army could attack the island. In 332 B.C., Alexander conquered the island city and burned it to the ground. The prophecies of Tyre's destruction were fulfilled in every detail as Alexander annihilated this "power," its riches, fleet of ships, commerce, and fortifications (cf. Ezek. 26—28).

Alexander the Great then traveled south to fight Egypt. As he advanced, he destroyed four of the five cities of Philistia: Ashkelon, Gaza, Ekron, and Ashdod (Zech. 9:5–6). Gath was omitted from the list, since Judah had already destroyed it (2 Chr. 26:6).

Ashkelon feared attack, and rightfully so, for Alexander annihilated the city's population (Zech. 9:5). Gaza anguished over the loss of its king, especially when Alexander replaced him with a Grecian governor (v. 5). Ekron had expected Tyre to come to its aid, but this was impossible since Alexander had already destroyed it. Ashdod would become a city of mixed nationalities after its destruction (v. 6).

With their demise, God eradicated the national pride and arrogance of these four Philistine cities and their idolatrous practices. God would "take away the blood from his mouth, and the abominations from between his teeth. But he who remains, even he shall be for our God, and shall be like a leader in Judah, and Ekron like a Jebusite" (v. 7). In other words, God would stop the practice of eating unclean animals (along with their blood) that had been sacrificed to idols. The people who survived ceased their idolatry and were absorbed into Israel. A similar absorption took place among the Jebusites after David defeated them and captured Zion.

Jerusalem Delivered

In contrast to these nations, Jerusalem would be spared. Humanly speaking, there is no good reason why Alexander should have spared Jerusalem. In fact, he was on his way to conquer the city. He had sent a messenger to Jerusalem requiring the tribute it paid to Persia be transferred to him, but the high priest refused to comply, not wanting to break his oath to Persia.

Jerusalem survived because God promised to protect the city from Alexander. Prophesying directly through Zechariah, the Lord said, "I will camp around My house because of [against or from] the army, because of [against] him who passes by and him who returns. No more shall an oppressor pass through them, for now I have seen with My eyes" (v. 8).

The words *My house* (v. 8) are a metonymy for the "land, Temple, and people of Israel." In his conquest of the Middle East, Alexander's marauding forces passed Jerusalem on the way to Egypt and returned via the same route without ever invading the city. Jerusalem's deliverance can be attributed directly to God's divine protection. The Lord promised to encamp around the city, and He did (2:5).

Ancient historian Flavius Josephus, in his *Antiquities of the Jews,* recorded how Jerusalem, humanly speaking, survived:

> And when he understood that he was not far from the
> city, he went out in procession with the priests and the
> multitude of the citizens. The procession was venerable and
> the manner of it different from that of other nations. . . .
> And when the Phoenicians and the Chaldeans that [who]
> followed him thought they should have liberty to plunder
> the city and torment the high priest to death, which the
> king's displeasure fairly promised them, the very reverse of
> it happened; for Alexander, when he saw the multitude at a
> distance, in white garments, while the priests stood clothed
> with fine linen, and the high priest in purple and scarlet
> clothing, with his mitre on his head, having the golden plate
> whereon the name of God was engraved, he approached by
> himself, and adored that name, and first saluted the high
> priest. The Jews also did all together, with one voice, salute
> Alexander, and encompass him about; whereupon the kings
> of Syria and the rest were surprised at what Alexander had
> done, and supposed him disordered in his mind. However,
> Parmenio alone went up to him, and asked him how it came
> to pass that, when all others adored him, he should adore
> the high priest of the Jews? To whom he replied, "I did not
> adore him, but that God who hath honored him with his
> high priesthood; for I saw this very person in a dream, in
> this very habit, when I was at Dios in Macedonia, who,
> when I was considering with myself how I might obtain the
> dominion of Asia, exhorted me to make no delay but boldly
> to pass over the sea thither, for that he would conduct my
> army, and would give me the dominion over the Persians;
> whence it is that, having seen no other in that habit, and
> now seeing this person in it, and remembering that vision
> and the exhortation which I had in my dream, I believe
> that I bring this army under the Divine conduct, and shall
> therewith conquer Darius, and destroy the power of the
> Persians, and that all things will succeed according to what
> is in my own mind" (11.8.5).

In other words, Jaddua the high priest heard that Alexander was on his way. Overwhelmed with fear, Jaddua ordered the city to sacrifice and pray to God. That night, Jaddua had a dream that he believed was from the Lord. He dreamed God instructed him to be courageous, decorate Jerusalem with wreaths, remove his priestly garments, and have the people dress in white. Then they were to march out of Jerusalem and welcome Alexander with open arms.

So Jaddua did just that. Josephus wrote that, when Alexander saw the procession, he prostrated himself before the high priest. Alexander's officers questioned whether he had gone insane. Alexander replied that he had seen this person in a dream, dressed as he was now, before beginning his conquest of Asia. In the dream, Alexander was told to conquer with confidence and take dominion of Persia.

Alexander was escorted to Jerusalem by Jaddua. There he went to the Temple, offered sacrifices, and was shown from the book of Daniel that a Greek would swiftly destroy the Persian Empire. Alexander offered Jaddua whatever he desired. The high priest asked that Jerusalem be left to live in peace, abide by its own laws, and be exempt from paying tribute. Alexander granted the request.

Alexander the Great did visit Jerusalem during his conquest of the Middle East, but how much of Josephus' account is fact and how much is legend is uncertain. What is certain is that God kept His promise to give Jerusalem divine protection, resulting in its survival against Alexander the Great.

Jerusalem's Destiny

Zechariah 9:8 ends with this marvelous word from the Lord: "No more shall an oppressor [taskmaster or slave driver] pass through them, for now I have seen with My eyes." In other words, God promises to watch over the Jewish people. His "eye" has seen Jerusalem's distress and destruction throughout the centuries, and there will come a day when He will allow it no more. Unfortunately, that day has not yet arrived.

After Alexander's death, Jerusalem suffered at the hands of many tyrants, especially the infamous Antiochus Epiphanes (Dan. 11:21–35). Antiochus was a Syrian king who desecrated the Temple by offering a pig on the altar (168 B.C.). Then he subjugated the people ruthlessly. Titus, a Roman general, destroyed both Jerusalem and Herod's Temple in A.D. 70.

Jesus prophesied, "Jerusalem will be trampled by Gentiles until the times of the Gentiles are fulfilled" (Lk. 21:24). Today some believe that, since Israel recaptured Jerusalem during the Six-Day War in 1967 and it is now under Israel's control, the "times of the Gentiles" has ended. This teaching is fallacious and not taught in God's Word.

It is clear from Scripture the "times of the Gentiles" began with the capture of Jerusalem under King Nebuchadnezzar of Babylon, as described in 2 Chronicles 36:1–21. The "times of the Gentiles" is spelled out in Daniel 2 when Nebuchadnezzar dreamed about a great image. God gave Daniel the interpretation, outlining the course of Gentile control of Jerusalem that would last until the Second Coming of the Messiah. This prophecy will ultimately come to fruition when the Messiah Himself protects Israel in the Millennial Kingdom. He will take control of Jerusalem and set up His Kingdom rule and reign. The New Testament confirms this fact when it says, "He [Jesus Christ] will be great. . . and the Lord God will give Him the throne of His father David" (Lk. 1:32). Then Jerusalem's oppression by the nations of the world will finally be terminated.

You might ask, "Why spend so much time on Alexander the Great's conquest?" It is important to see how Alexander's victory prepared the Near East for the Messiah's First Coming. Alexander encouraged his soldiers to marry women in the areas he conquered and educate them in Greek law, language, and culture. Greek became the lingua franca of the Middle East. Romans spoke Greek as a second language. Eleven of the Lord's disciples spent much of their lives near the Sea of Galilee, around which bordered the Greek cities of the Decapolis. With Greek manuscripts in hand, the apostles spread the gospel of the Messiah to the farthest parts of a Greek-speaking world.

Thus we see another illustration of God's sovereign hand organizing, orchestrating, and overruling in the course of history to prepare for the advent of the Messiah.

CHAPTER 11

The Messianic King

Zechariah 9:9–17

The Jewish people survived Alexander's conquest because God kept His promise to protect the city (Zech. 9:8). After Alexander's death, however, cruel Grecian and Roman rulers subjugated Israel while the nation hoped for deliverance by a military Messiah.

Zechariah revealed that a Messianic King was coming to deliver Israel, both physically and spiritually; and Zechariah described how the Jewish people would recognize Him.

Messiah Presented to Israel

The prophet began by announcing that Israel's King is coming to them:

Rejoice greatly, O daughter of Zion! Shout, O daughter of Jerusalem! Behold, your King is coming to you; He is just and having salvation, lowly and riding on a donkey, a colt, the foal of a donkey (v. 9).

Both Judaism and Christianity embrace this verse as a reference to Israel's Messiah riding victoriously into Jerusalem. Christianity sees this prophecy fulfilled on what is traditionally called Palm Sunday (Mt. 21:4–5), whereas Judaism believes it will be fulfilled when the Messiah delivers Israel and establishes His Kingdom in Jerusalem.

Zechariah did not call Him "a" King, but "your" King (Zech. 9:9). He is Israel's righteous Savior-King, its long-awaited Messiah. Such news should have evoked great joy in Israel. Verse 9 personifies the people of Jerusalem as a young woman commanded to shout with ecstatic joy at the news of the nation's coming King. When Zechariah presented this revelation, there was no king on Israel's throne, nor will there be one from the royal line of David until the Messiah comes. Zechariah then revealed three characteristics of the Messianic King.

First, "He is just," that is, righteous by nature in conformity to God's standard of morality and ethics. Messiah's righteousness will be manifested in both His character and reign. The Messiah is righteous because, at His First Advent, He was supernaturally virgin-born (Isa. 7:14; Mt. 1:23), possessing no sin nature. The same cannot be said of any other king who ever lived, especially Alexander the Great, who was wicked, capricious, violent, and unjust.

Second, the Messiah will be revealed as "having salvation," or endowed with salvation, showing Himself as a Savior-Deliverer. This was the reason for His First Coming, as He bore the guilt and paid the penalty for man's sin. Today He is able to save completely and forever all who come to God through Him because He is the "author of eternal salvation" (Heb. 5:9; cf. 7:25). At His Second Coming, a remnant in Israel will be redeemed and delivered (Zech. 12:10; Rom. 11:26). Such was not the case with Alexander the Great, who destroyed and subjugated those he conquered.

Third, He is "lowly" in His soul and outward state. The Hebrew word for "lowly" means more than being humble or meek; it refers to one brought low by affliction, poverty, persecution, or bereavement (Ps. 22:6–7; Isa. 53:3–4; Mt. 8:20; 11:29; 2 Cor. 8:9). It seems out of character to speak of the Messiah-King in such a paradoxical way, for kings exude pride and pomp.

This Messiah-King did not ride into Jerusalem on a horse but "on a donkey, a colt, the foal of a donkey." This prophecy was fulfilled in what is traditionally called the Triumphal Entry (Mt. 21:1–5). Early in Israel's history, a donkey was the animal on which kings and judges rode (Jud. 5:10; 10:4; 2 Sam. 16:1–2). By the time of Solomon, kings rode horses— symbols of pride, pomp, and power; plus they were instruments of self-reliance and strength in time of battle. Today the donkey is regarded as a lowly beast of burden.

Jesus instructed His disciples to fetch not only the young donkey but the mother as well. The donkey was a young colt, never ridden and still running behind its mother. Jesus' royal entrance into Jerusalem on the back of a young, untrained donkey symbolized His coming in peace and humility and sheds light on Zechariah 9:9 in three ways. First, it is a Messianic prophecy. Second, Jesus is the long-awaited Messiah mentioned in this verse. Third, this prophecy was fulfilled at Jesus' First Coming.

Zechariah then took a gigantic leap from the Messiah's First Advent

(v. 9) to His Second (v. 10). The Messiah rode humbly into Jerusalem at His First Advent. At His Second, He will descend from heaven on a white horse as Israel's Redeemer-King to inaugurate His worldwide Kingdom rule.

Zechariah gave Israel reasons to rejoice over the Messiah's Second Coming:

> *I will cut off the chariot from Ephraim and the horse from*
> *Jerusalem; the battle bow shall be cut off. He shall speak*
> *peace to the nations; His dominion shall be "from sea to sea,*
> *and from the River to the ends of the earth"* (v. 10).

First, Messiah will establish worldwide peace. Second, He will destroy the weapons of war. "The chariot from Ephraim," "the horse from Jerusalem," and "the battle bow" all speak of weapons used in ancient warfare. These will be destroyed and the materials converted into implements of peace (Isa. 2:4; 9:4–5). Third, Ephraim and Judah will be united into a single Kingdom of peace (Ezek. 37:15–22) for the first time since the days of Solomon. Fourth, He will establish peace among all nations of the world, something not experienced in the annals of human history. Fifth, His reign and rule will begin in Jerusalem but shall cover the earth (Ps. 72:8–11).

A striking contrast can be made between the Messiah and Alexander the Great. Alexander was a depraved monarch who came riding on a horse in pomp and power with military brutality to make war, smiting and subjugating nations. Conversely, Messiah is the God-Man who, at His First Coming, rode into Jerusalem in humility and peace, presenting Himself as Israel's long-awaited King of righteousness and peace. At His Second Coming, the Messiah will establish a righteous Kingdom of universal peace and prosperity.

Messiah's Promise to Israel

Before the Messiah establishes His Kingdom, He must deliver and restore the nation of Israel: "As for you also, because of the blood of your covenant, I will set your prisoners free from the waterless pit" (Zech. 9:11). God will deliver the Jewish people on the basis of the blood covenants He made with Israel: the Abrahamic and Mosaic Covenants (Gen. 15:8–21; Ex. 24:5–8). The "waterless pit" refers to an empty cistern that functions like a prison, like the one where Joseph was incarcerated by his brothers

(Gen. 37:24). The word *prisoners* may have been an immediate reference to Jewish exiles freed from Babylon, but the prophecy ultimately refers to the regathering of the Jewish people at the end of the Great Tribulation.

The exiles in Babylon were called "prisoners of hope" because God promised them deliverance after their 70-year captivity (Jer. 25:11-12): "Return to the stronghold, you prisoners of hope. Even today I declare that I will restore double to you" (Zech. 9:12).

A remnant of Jewish people did return from captivity to their "stronghold" (Jerusalem) after the 70 years were fulfilled. The Lord declared He would "restore double" blessing to them—a promise with greater fulfillment in the Kingdom Age (v. 12).

In verse 13, the Lord pictures Himself as a mighty warrior using Judah as His "bow" and Ephraim (the northern kingdom) as His "arrow" to defeat His and Israel's enemies. Power was (and will be) given to Israel, "like the sword of a mighty man," to destroy its enemies, especially "Greece," but also its enemies at the end of the Tribulation (v. 13; 14:14).

Many scholars say the word *Greece* refers to the terrible period of Grecian persecution under Antiochus IV (Epiphanes). Antiochus desecrated the Temple by sacrificing a pig on the altar. He also tortured Jewish people and forbade them to practice their religion. An Israelite family led by Mattathias revolted against Antiochus' domination. In a three-year conflict with Antiochus, Mattathias's son Judah liberated Jerusalem, cleansed the Temple from heathen desecration, and reestablished Jewish worship (168–165 B.C.). The family became known as the Maccabees, from the Hebrew word for "hammer." The Jewish holiday of Hanukkah (Feast of the Dedication) was established to commemorate this event.

Messiah's Protection of Israel

In verses 14–15, the Lord is depicted as a mighty warrior ready to do battle with His enemies while hovering over Israel to protect it:

> *Then the LORD will be seen over them, and His arrow will go forth like lightning. The Lord GOD will blow the trumpet, and go with whirlwinds from the south. The LORD of hosts will defend them.*

He will marshal His troops with the sound of the "trumpet," and His "arrow" will strike the enemy at the speed of lightning. The Lord will sweep away His enemies with hurricane force like "whirlwinds from the south."

Verse 15 says, "They shall devour and subdue with slingstones. They shall drink and roar as if with wine; they shall be filled with blood like basins, like the corners of the altar." Commentators interpret this two ways. Some teach it refers to Israel devouring its enemies with God's protective help. Others teach the verse describes a banquet to celebrate God's victory over His and Israel's enemies. The latter interpretation seems best in this context. Those celebrating will trample the "slingstones," or spent weapons, of their enemy. Israel will roar in joyful exuberance like a person drunk with wine and filled with food from a victory banquet. The text simply states banquet provisions will be plentiful, and participants will be filled with drink like sacrificial basins and with meat like the corners of the sacrificial altar.

This prophecy was partially fulfilled when the Maccabees defeated Antiochus Epiphanes. But its ultimate fulfillment will occur when the Messiah's enemies are destroyed at His Second Coming.

Messiah's Provision for Israel

Zechariah revealed what will take place at the Messiah's Second Coming. First, the Lord will bring spiritual life, or "save," the remnant of Jewish people who survive the Tribulation (v. 16; 12:10—13:1, 9; Rom. 11:26). Then the Lord will shepherd "the flock of His people" as a shepherd does his sheep, guaranteeing Israel safety and security (Zech. 9:16). He will look on redeemed Israel as a sparkling stone—His treasured possession—that will glitter "like the jewels of a crown" (v. 16; cf. Ex. 19:5) in the Millennial Kingdom and set Israel as a "banner," or standard, over His glorious Kingdom (Zech. 9:16).

In that day, the great splendor of the Lord's "goodness" and "beauty" will shine throughout Israel (v. 17). Sowed seed will produce a great harvest because of abundant rain. (See Zechariah 10:1.) "Grain shall make the young men thrive, and new wine the young women" (9:17). Grain and wine symbolize productivity, plenty, and prosperity that all will enjoy during the Kingdom Age.

There is an innate longing in Jewish hearts for the coming of their Messianic King. When the Messiah comes, He will bring redemption, execute deliverance, and establish His Kingdom of universal peace.

CHAPTER 12

Israel's Shepherd

Zechariah 10:1–12

In the previous chapter, the Lord is pictured as a Shepherd who saves Israel, and Israel becomes "the flock of His people" (Zech. 9:16). Israel's redemption will take place when the nation receives the Messiah at His Second Advent.

Chapter 10 continues the theme of Israel's redemption and restoration. Messiah appears as a compassionate, caring Shepherd who will lead the flock of Israel, vanquish Israel's enemies, restore and reunite the 12 tribes, and shower the nation with prosperity.

Israel's Ruling Shepherds

The temporal blessings promised in Zechariah 9:17 are expounded upon in this chapter. These blessings come from God's hand, not from the idols mentioned in 10:2. Zechariah commanded Israel, "Ask the LORD for rain in the time of the latter rain" (v. 1). The "latter rain" comes in late spring (March–April) and is essential for Israel's crops.

Those asking for rain are assured the request will be granted: "The LORD will make flashing clouds [lightning flashes]; He will give them showers of rain, grass in the field for everyone" (v. 1). Notice, if the men of Israel will simply make their requests known to God, He will grant all who ask for rain the amount necessary for a productive harvest.

In the past, the Israelites were led astray by ungodly leaders who failed to direct them to seek God for His help. Instead, their leaders directed them to idols that had no power. Zechariah rightly said that those who divined with idols were full of deception: "For the idols speak delusion; the diviners envision lies, and tell false dreams; they comfort in vain" (v. 2).

These idols (Hebrew, *teraphim*) were household gods used to "predict" the future. People who practiced such divining were deluded and predicted ungodly lies. They were like fortune-tellers who offered false hope. Their predictions were empty promises, providing no comfort to the expectant Israelite. The Lord had warned Israel not to seek guidance through the abomination of divination (Dt. 18:10–12).

The deception of Israel's diviners carried consequences. First, the people wandered away from the truth: "Therefore the people wend their way like sheep" (Zech. 10:2). Sheep without a shepherd wander and become lost, unable to find their way back to the flock.

Second, Israel was wounded: "They are in trouble because there is no shepherd" (v. 2). The Hebrew word for "trouble" connotes being browbeaten or humbled in the journey through life. The imperfect tense indicates that Israel's trouble still exists today and will continue until the Messiah removes the nation's sin at His coming.

Third, many of Israel's shepherds were worthless. The word for "shepherd" refers to Israel's kings, priests, and prophets—the men who led the nation (v. 2). Under Roman occupation, for example, Israel's political leaders were corrupt. The nation was described as "sheep having no shepherd" (Mt. 9:36)—a condition that will exist until the Messiah comes to shepherd the nation.

Fourth, the Lord's wrath will burn against those who abuse the flock of Israel: "My anger is kindled against the shepherds, and I will punish the goatherds" (Zech. 10:3). God's anger burned like a kindling fire against Israel's apostate leaders. The goatherds are wicked leaders in high places, both Jewish and Gentile, who seek to subjugate and shepherd the flock of Israel for their own profit.

Israel's Righteous Shepherd

In contrast to Israel's false shepherds, "the LORD of hosts will visit His flock, the house of Judah, and will make them as His royal horse in the battle" (v. 3). In other words, God will take faithful shepherds from His sheepfold in Judah and turn them into His strong army to overthrow the ungodly Gentiles who persecute the Jewish people prior to the Messiah's return.

Zechariah used four phrases in verse 4, each beginning with the words *from him,* which refer to Judah, to describe how Israel's righteous Messianic Shepherd will help the nation.

(1) From him comes [is] the cornerstone. The word *cornerstone* is a Messianic title. Throughout Scripture, the Messiah is identified as a stone: a stone of stumbling (Isa. 8:14; Rom. 9:32–33), a smitten stone (Ex. 17:6; 1 Cor. 10:4), a smiting stone at His Second Coming (Dan. 2:34–35), and a rejected stone that became the chief cornerstone (Ps. 118:22–23; Mt. 21:42). A cornerstone was the boulder laid at the corner of a building where two walls met. It was the principal stone of a foundation, giving a structure stability and strength. The apostle Paul identified the "chief cornerstone" as Jesus the Messiah (Eph. 2:20). With the Messiah as the cornerstone, Israel's leaders should not fear the nation's enemies. The complete fulfillment of this prophecy will be at the Messiah's Second Coming, when He will endow Israel's leaders with the needed strength and power to conquer their enemies.

(2) From him [is] the tent peg. A tent peg holds a tent cord taut. In Isaiah 22:15–25, this imagery is used of Eliakim, the son of Hilkiah, who replaced Shebna as administrator of David's house in Jerusalem. Eliakim was like a tent peg because he brought stability to the house of Judah (vv. 22–23). In Zechariah, the term refers to the Messiah, whose leadership, like a deeply driven peg, will bring support, stability, and security to the nation of Judah.

(3) From him [is] the battle bow. The battle bow symbolizes strength for military conquest (2 Ki. 13:17). The Messiah is the great Conqueror and Avenger against His and Israel's enemies (Ps. 45:5; Rev. 19:11–16). When He returns, He will be like a weapon in the hand of God the Father to smite nations that have come against Israel. Not only will He give Israel military strength to vanquish its enemies, but He will also give its new leadership the strength and stability to defend the nation under His rule.

(4) From him [is] every ruler together. The Messiah will empower Judah to drive out every oppressor from Israel. Sensing the Lord's strength, the people of Judah will be

forged into an army of "mighty men," or strong warriors, who will defeat their enemies and trample them into the "mire of the streets" (Zech. 10: 5). The cavalry of Gentiles will be overthrown and "put to shame," confused and embarrassed by Judah's victory and subjugation (v. 5). This will take place prior to the establishment of the Millennial Kingdom.

The Lord will have mercy on the entire nation of Israel:

I will strengthen the house of Judah, and I will save the house of Joseph. I will bring them back, because I have mercy on them. They shall be as though I had not cast them aside (v. 6).

Judah represents the southern kingdom, and Joseph represents the 10 tribes of the northern kingdom that separated from Judah after Solomon's death (931 B.C). Israel will again be forged into one nation due to the Lord's mercy—His unbroken, unconditional love for the nation. Israel's worldwide restoration will be comprehensive and complete, as if its division and exile had never taken place. The Lord will forgive and forget Israel's sin, and the nation will enjoy a new communication with Him. For, as God said, "I am the LORD their God, and I will hear them" (v. 6); that is, He will listen to their requests and answer quickly.

Ephraim, also representing the 10 tribes, will be restored and empowered "like a mighty man" (v. 7). The tribes' reinstatement and renewal will produce great rejoicing: "And their heart shall rejoice as if with wine. Yes, their children shall see it and be glad" (v. 7). In other words, children will rejoice along with their parents.

Israel's Redemption Secured

As a shepherd uses the shrill sound of a pipe to signal his scattered sheep to come (Jud. 5:16), so the Lord will whistle His scattered sheep back to their land: "I will whistle for them and gather them, for I will redeem them; and they shall increase as they once increased" (Zech. 10:8). His call will be to redeem Jewish people from sin and separate them from the nations into which they were scattered. Since Israel's exile, its population has remained small (Dt. 28:62). But after its return, the Jewish population will increase greatly, as it did during the captivity in Egypt.

Israel's dispersion was God's doing: "I will sow [scatter] them among the peoples, and they shall remember Me in far countries; they shall live, together with their children, and they shall return" (Zech. 10:9; cf. Lev. 26:40–42; Dt. 28:63–64; 30:1–3). While living in the Diaspora, Jewish people will "remember" the Lord—that is, turn to Him in repentance (Zech. 13:1). Then God will regather them, along with their children, and "they shall live," or experience a life of spiritual and physical blessing in Israel. Although Jewish people are experiencing some blessing there today, the fulfillment of this prophecy will come during the Millennium: "I will also bring them back from the land of Egypt, and gather them from Assyria. I will bring them into the land of Gilead and Lebanon, until no more room is found for them" (10:10).

God will bring them back from "Egypt" and "Assyria," lands that represent the major areas of Israel's captivities (v. 10). Scripture mentions Assyria in the north and Egypt in the south because they were Israel's most formidable enemies. These nations represent any world power that would hamper the regathering of the Jewish people to their land. Proud Assyria's prestige will be broken, and Egypt's scepter (a symbol of the nation's governmental authority to obstruct and oppress Israel) will be taken away.

The Jewish people will take up residence in the land of "Gilead [east of the Jordan River] and Lebanon [northwest of present-day Israel]." This land was promised to Israel in the Abrahamic Covenant. (See Genesis 15:18–21.) So numerous will be the returnees to Israel that "no more room is found for them" (Zech. 10:10).

The Lord "shall pass through the sea with affliction [sea of trouble], and strike the waves of the sea: All the depths of the River shall dry up. Then the pride of Assyria shall be brought down, and the scepter of Egypt shall depart" (v. 11). In other words, the Lord will go before the Jewish people to remove every obstacle and barrier that would hamper their worldwide return. Their deliverance will be similar to when the Lord parted the Red Sea to make a way for Israel to escape the Egyptian army (Ex. 14:21–31). Enemies of the Jewish people, like Egypt and Assyria, are used figuratively to show that Israel's most formidable oppressors will be removed.

God alone supplies the Jewish people with strength to return: "'So I will strengthen them in the LORD, and they shall walk up and down in His name,' says the LORD" (Zech. 10:12). At the Messiah's Second Coming, the redeemed remnant of Jewish people who return to their land will live in obedience to the Lord. Strong and secure in Him, a redeemed Israel will walk throughout the world as priests and ministers of their God, witnessing to the glory of the Lord with power and great zeal (Isa. 61:6).

What a picture of Israel's redemption and restoration! Israel's false shepherds will be replaced by the Messiah of Israel, its true Shepherd. He will deliver Israel from all of its enemies, visible and invisible, and bring to fruition these words: "I will place salvation in Zion, for Israel My glory" (46:13).

CHAPTER 13

Israel's Rejected Shepherd

Zechariah 11:1–17

In Zechariah 9 and 10, the Messiah was revealed as a compassionate Shepherd who will someday reunite and restore Israel. The revelation greatly encouraged Israel, but the good news was quickly dispelled in chapter 11.

The prophecies of chapter 11 cover three themes: the destruction of Israel, along with its national shepherds; Israel's rejection of its Messiah, the true Shepherd, at His First Advent; and Israel's acceptance of the worthless shepherd during the Great Tribulation. Two prophecies were fulfilled in the centuries after Zechariah's prediction; one is yet to be fulfilled before Israel experiences the Millennial Kingdom blessings promised in the earlier chapters.

The Wailing Shepherds

In poetic language, Zechariah called on Lebanon to open its doors to a devastating "fire" (symbol of an invading army) that will sweep down from the north and destroy the majestic cedars of Lebanon (Zech. 11:1). The army will also devour the strong oaks and rich pasture lands of Bashan northeast of Lebanon and the "thick forest" lining the Jordan River in the south (vv. 2–3). The trees are metaphors for the area's proud kings, on whom the judgment will fall. This event, the fire of God's judgment, will not only destroy the land, but also the ungodly kings and their kingdoms from Lebanon in the north to Israel in the south.

The call goes out for the cypresses and oaks to lament the tragic destruction of the cedars because they will be destroyed as well. The lowly shepherds are to lament the loss of their lush, green pastures, and lions will roar at the destruction of their lairs and food supply (vv. 2–3).

Commentators disagree on the reason for and time of God's devastating judgment, but both are made clear in the verses that follow.

The reason is Israel's rejection of the true Shepherd, Jesus the Messiah. After Israel's leadership rejected Him, Jesus said, "See! Your house is left to you desolate" (Mt. 23:38). The time of this destruction came 38 years after Jesus' crucifixion, in A.D. 70. Titus the Roman invaded Judah and destroyed Jerusalem and Herod's Temple. Thousands of Jewish people perished. Jerusalem became subservient to Rome, and the survivors were enslaved. In time, their descendants were dispersed worldwide and have suffered unbelievable persecution wherever they have traveled for the past 2,000 years.

The Worthy Shepherd

The Lord commissioned Zechariah to play the role of a worthy shepherd to illustrate the nature of the true Shepherd, Jesus the Messiah. The prophet was told, "Feed the flock for slaughter," or fatten Israel, destined to be butchered by its wicked leaders and the Roman Empire:

> *Thus says the LORD my God, "Feed the flock for slaughter,*
> *whose owners slaughter them and feel no guilt; those who*
> *sell them say, 'Blessed be the LORD, for I am rich'; and their*
> *shepherds do not pity them"* (Zech. 11:4–5).

Israel's wicked shepherds had no compassion on the people and simply used them for financial gain. These leaders functioned like merchants who raised sheep to be sold and butchered for their fleeces and meat. They dealt ruthlessly with the flock of Israel, showing no pity or compassion and feeling no guilt for their actions. In fact, they even believed their subsequent financial gain was a blessing from God.

One author put it well: "Herod, king of Judea, was utterly callous and brutal and entirely subservient to Rome. The high priestly family later exploited and enriched themselves at the expense of the people and was hated by them for their rapacity and violence."[1] To make matters worse, they had the audacity to believe their enrichment was a blessing from the Lord.

Israel's greatest tragedy was to experience the withdrawal of God's pity:

> *"For I will no longer pity the inhabitants of the land," says*
> *the LORD. "But indeed I will give everyone into his neighbor's*

---

[1] Nathan J. Stone, *Jehovah Remembers: Studies in Zechariah, Part 2* (Chicago: Moody Bible Institute, 1966), 15.

hand and into the hand of his king. They shall attack the
land, and I will not deliver them from their hand" (v. 6).

Thus Rome laid siege to Jerusalem, and Israel became the possession of Caesar. Continuing in his role as a shepherd, Zechariah said, "So I fed the flock for slaughter, in particular the poor of the flock" (v. 7). He fed the nation by giving it the Word of God as presented in this book—a symbolic act of what the Messiah would do at His First Advent. It was the poor who responded to the gospel message of the Messiah, not Israel's king, priests, or prophets (Mt. 11:5; 1 Cor. 1:26–29).

A shepherd carried two staffs: a club to ward off wild animals and a crook to retrieve sheep from difficult or dangerous places. So Zechariah took two staffs: "The one I called Beauty [grace], and the other I called Bonds [union]; and I fed the flock" (Zech. 11:7). The words *grace* and *union* describe Zechariah's objective as a shepherd and aptly symbolize the Messiah's ministry at His First Advent. As Israel's true Shepherd, the Messiah manifested God's love and grace to the nation in hopes that it would repent of its sin and be restored and unified under God.

Abruptly, Zechariah announced that he "dismissed the three shepherds in one month" and declared, "My soul loathed them, and their soul also abhorred me" (v. 8). Although the three shepherds are not identified, most conservative commentators see them as the kings, priests, and false prophets of Israel. These leaders not only rejected Zechariah's ministry but also their Messiah at His First Coming. Zechariah's soul was impatient with, or "loathed," these evil leaders as much as they loathed him—a picture of God's impatience with these unrepentant shepherds who mistreated all the prophets who brought them the truth of God's Word.

Continuing in his role as a shepherd, Zechariah abandoned his sheep, something totally out of character for a shepherd. The prophet said, "I will not feed you. Let what is dying die, and what is perishing perish. Let those that are left eat each other's flesh" (v. 9). In other words, God turned Israel over to the judgment predicted for it. This prophecy came true literally when Jewish people actually devoured one another during the Roman siege in A.D. 70 (cf. Dt. 28:54–57). At this point, the words of the Messiah ring in our ears:

O Jerusalem, Jerusalem, the one who kills the prophets and
stones those who are sent to her! How often I wanted to

gather your children together, as a hen gathers her chicks under her wings, but you were not willing! See! Your house is left to you desolate" (Mt. 23:37–38).

The prophet then took the staff called Beauty "and cut it in two," symbolizing God "break[ing] the covenant which [He] had made with all the peoples" (Zech. 11:10). What covenant is this? It is not the unconditional covenants made with Abraham and David, but the Mosaic Covenant that God conditionally made with Israel. Israel had already broken this covenant; thus God broke the staff of Beauty—that is, removed His protective grace from the nation, opening the way to destruction by its enemies. Watching Zechariah break his staff, "the poor of the flock" realized this act "was the word of the LORD" (v. 11).

Zechariah concluded his role as shepherd by asking Israel to put a price on his service: "If it is agreeable to you, give me my wages; and if not, refrain" (v. 12). The Israelites saw little value in Zechariah's shepherding, so "they weighed out" for his wages "thirty pieces of silver" (v. 12). This was a great insult to the prophet, as 30 pieces of silver was the amount paid for a slave who had been gored by an ox (Ex. 21:32). The Lord called the sum a "princely price" (Zech. 11:13)—a sarcastic statement concerning the low value placed on the prophet's service.

The Lord instructed Zechariah, "Throw it to the potter," whereupon the prophet "took the thirty pieces of silver and threw them into the house of the LORD for the potter" (v. 13). Throwing the money to a potter (one of the lowest classes of workers) in the Temple was the same as saying "Throw the worthless wage away."

The fulfillment of this prophecy is recorded in the New Testament when Judas Iscariot, guilty of rejecting and betraying Jesus the Messiah for 30 pieces of silver, cast down the blood money in the Temple. The chief priests could not accept blood money for Temple use but took the silver and purchased a potter's field outside Jerusalem in which to bury strangers (Mt. 26:14–16; 27:3–10).

Now Zechariah said, "I cut in two my other staff, Bonds, that I might break the brotherhood between Judah and Israel" (Zech. 11:14). This staff symbolized the religious, civil, and social union between Judah and Israel. Cutting the staff into pieces symbolized Israel's destruction in two ways. First, in the siege of Jerusalem, internal division and fighting broke out among the Jewish people and their leaders, threatening their survival from within. Second, this internal strife made it much easier for the Roman 10th Legion to breach the city's walls and destroy both it and its people.

The Wicked Shepherd

The scene abruptly switches from Israel's destruction to the day when Israel will make a covenant with the Antichrist and eventually become enslaved as his flock during the Great Tribulation (cf. Dan. 9:27; Jn. 5:43). Since Israel rejected God's chosen Shepherd, He will now place a worthless shepherd (the Antichrist) over them.

The Lord commanded Zechariah, "Take for yourself the implements of a foolish shepherd" (Zech. 11:15). The word *foolish* speaks of a person who is morally perverse and, in this context, has no concern for the Jewish people who are "cut off." No concern indeed! "He will eat [their] flesh . . . and tear their hooves in pieces" (v. 16). True to God's prophetic Word, the foolish shepherd will be the very opposite of the true Shepherd; he will viciously and greedily destroy every part of Israel as one would devour a lamb—even its hooves.

The doom of this wicked shepherd is sealed and will come quickly. "A sword shall be against his arm and against his right eye; his arm shall completely wither, and his right eye shall be totally blinded" (v. 17). That is, his arm—which should be used to defend the sheep—and his right eye—which should watch over the flock to keep it from danger—will be destroyed by the sword. The Antichrist's destruction will come by the hand of the Messiah (the true Shepherd) at His Second Coming (2 Th. 2:8; Rev. 19:19–20).

For the past 2,000 years, Jewish people have suffered because of the nation's alienation from the Messiah and because of belligerent, satanically inspired Gentile persecution. Knowing what awaits the nation in the future, Israel needs our support, love, and, above all, our prayers as never before.

CHAPTER 14

Salvation of Israel

Zechariah 12:1–14

Will Israel survive the hatred and unceasing persecution that has plagued it for centuries? Although it faces a cauldron of unrelenting conflict, Israel will survive the world's attempts to annihilate it.

The last three chapters of Zechariah form a single prophecy that reveals the struggle Israel will face to stay alive. This prophecy describes a series of events that will culminate with the Messiah's return, Israel's salvation, and the establishment of His Kingdom on Earth.

The prophet's message is described as the "burden [oracle] of the word of the LORD against [concerning] Israel" (Zech. 12:1). The word *burden* refers to something heavy, a load to be lifted. In context, the "burden" is a weighty message from the Lord concerning (1) a yet-future siege against Jerusalem and (2) the eventual salvation of Israel.

Before unveiling the prophecy in chapter 12, Zechariah reminds us that no force in the universe can deter or divert God's plan and purpose for Israel. This is assurance from "the LORD, who stretches out the heavens, lays the foundation of the earth, and forms the spirit of man within him" (v. 1).

God did not create the universe like a clock that was wound and left to run on its own. To the contrary, His omniscience and omnipotence continue to maintain the movement of everything in the universe, including creating and guiding man's spirit within him. Thus God is actively involved in bringing to consummation His planned destiny for Jerusalem and the Jewish people.

The setting for the fulfillment of these prophecies is *in that day,* a phrase used 16 times in the last three chapters. It refers to the Day of the Lord, a time of God's wrath and blessing that extends from the beginning of the future seven-year Tribulation to the end of the Millennial Kingdom.

The Siege of Jerusalem

Any nation that invades Jerusalem during the Day of the Lord will suffer severe judgment. God declared the following:

Behold, I will make Jerusalem a cup of drunkenness to all the surrounding peoples, when they lay siege against Judah and Jerusalem. And it shall happen in that day that I will make Jerusalem a very heavy stone for all peoples; all who would heave it away will surely be cut in pieces, though all nations of the earth are gathered against it (vv. 2–3).

God is saying that the nations that will attack Jerusalem will drink the full cup of His wrath. Every invading army will become disoriented, like an intoxicated person who reels under the influence of alcohol. In their stupefied conditions, the armies will stumble, fall, and become immobilized in battle.

Likewise, Jerusalem is compared to "a very heavy [burdensome] stone" that weighs too much to "heave…away." And it will "cut in pieces [lacerate]" anyone who tries (v. 3). In other words, those who attack Jerusalem will rupture, injure, and lacerate themselves. In spite of this awesome, detailed warning, "all nations of the earth" will come against Jerusalem in the Day of the Lord (v. 3).

As the battle progresses, said the Lord, "I will strike every horse with confusion, and its rider with madness; I will open My eyes on the house of Judah, and will strike every horse of the peoples with blindness" (v. 4). God will smite the horses with "confusion" (panic) and "blindness" and the riders with "madness" (consternation). Because of Israel's sin, God brought madness, blindness, and confusion of heart to the nation (Dt. 28:28; cf. 1–68). God will use the same type of confusion to wipe out Israel's enemies. While the armies are being destroyed, the Lord's "eyes" will be on the house of Judah, divinely protecting the nation. (See Zechariah 3:9; 4:10; 9:8.)

The Strength of Judah

At the appointed time, the inhabitants of Jerusalem and Judah will turn to the Lord for strength: "And the governors [leaders] of Judah shall say in their heart, 'The inhabitants of Jerusalem are my strength in the

LORD of hosts, their God'" (12:5). That is, the inhabitants of Jerusalem will recognize "the LORD of hosts" as their strength to sustain them in the conflict. In the process, leaders and citizens alike will be empowered and fortified to resist and conquer their foes. Judah will realize that God alone secured its victory.

Zechariah used two similes in describing the strength given to the Jewish people. They will be "like a firepan [firepot] in the woodpile, and like a fiery torch in the sheaves; they shall devour all the surrounding peoples on the right hand and on the left" (v. 6). Jerusalem's attackers will be swiftly consumed like kindling wood ignited by a firepot full of hot coals or a pile of bound sheaves that is quickly incinerated by a fiery torch. In the midst of the battle, Jerusalem's inhabitants will not flee but will remain in their "own place—Jerusalem" (v. 6).

All Judah will survive the battle: "The LORD will save the tents of Judah first, so that the glory of the house of David and the glory of the inhabitants of Jerusalem shall not become greater than that of Judah" (v. 7). Those living in the rural areas of Jerusalem are delivered first because of their vulnerability, but all in Judah shall share equally in the glorious victory.

Jewish people will be given divine power that will shield and strengthen them during the conflict. The "feeble among them in that day shall be like David" (v. 8). David was Israel's great warrior-king. He was unbeatable in battle. Furthermore, "the house of David shall be like God, like the Angel of the LORD before them" (v. 8). Israel will be endowed with great power "like the Angel of the LORD" (the preincarnate Christ) who is the invincible Commander of the Lord's army. It was He who strengthened Israel to be victorious over its enemies (cf. Ex. 23:20; 32:34; 33:2; Josh. 5:13–15).

In that day, the Lord will "seek to destroy all the nations that come against Jerusalem" (Zech. 12:9). The word *seek* does not cast doubt on God's ability to destroy Jerusalem's enemies, nor does it question the success of His mission. To the contrary, *seek* means the Lord will give His undivided attention to seeking out and destroying any nation that will come against Jerusalem.

The Salvation of Jerusalem

At the Messiah's Second Advent, God will bring salvation to a remnant in Jerusalem:

> *And I will pour on the house of David and on the inhabitants of Jerusalem the Spirit of grace and supplication; then they will look on Me whom they pierced. Yes, they will mourn for Him as one mourns for his only son, and grieve for Him as one grieves for a firstborn* (v. 10).

The word *I* refers to the Lord who is doing the speaking. He is the Creator of the universe who pours out the "Spirit of grace" on Jerusalem by means of the Holy Spirit. Grace and supplication sum up the ministry of the Holy Spirit as He brings salvation to the inhabitants of Jerusalem (cf. Ezek. 37:14; 39:29; Joel 2:28–29). It is the Holy Spirit who bestows God's grace on a person or a nation.

In that day (the end-times climax of the seven-year Tribulation), the veil that has for centuries covered the eyes of Jewish people, with the exception of the believing remnant, will be lifted. Then, said the Lord, "They will look on Me whom they pierced" (Zech. 12:10). The word *they* refers to Jewish people upon whom the "Spirit of grace and supplication" is poured. The word *Me* refers to God, the One who is speaking. In context, this speaker is the divine Messiah.

For several reasons, Jewish scholars have been perplexed over this verse. First, the text says, "They will look upon Me whom they pierced." The word *pierced* (Hebrew, *daqar*) means to be "thrust through," normally by a sword or spear, usually resulting in a disgraceful and violent death. Since God is speaking, how could God be pierced, resulting in His death? Second, if God is pierced, how could Jewish people look to a dead God for salvation? The answer is found in Jesus the Messiah. He is not only divine but took on flesh and became a man. As a man, Jesus willingly tasted death by crucifixion to redeem sinful humanity; but three days later, He was resurrected.

Partial fulfillment of this text took place at Jesus' crucifixion. Roman soldiers hammered nails through Jesus' hands and feet and thrust a spear into His side. The historical event was clearly recorded in all four New Testament Gospels. The apostle John saw Jesus' crucifixion as a fulfillment of this text (Jn. 19:37). Although a Jewish mob called for Jesus to be crucified, Roman soldiers actually did the deed. Scripture clearly reveals that all humanity is responsible for Jesus' crucifixion (Acts 4:27–28).

When the Holy Spirit is poured out on Jerusalem, Jewish people will "look on" (look unto) their Messiah with trust and hope for salvation. This will result in individuals greatly mourning over their sin. Each will recognize that the "Me" in Zechariah 12:10 refers to his or her Savior and Lord, Jesus, the promised Messiah, who was rejected and pierced at His First Advent.

Every stratum of Israel's society will publicly and privately mourn over its sin. Zechariah illustrated the mourning in three ways. First, people "will mourn for Him as one mourns for his only son, and grieve for Him as one grieves for a firstborn" son (v. 10). The death of an only or firstborn son produces profound grief and elicits one of the deepest types of mourning in a Jewish family. Such mourning became a proverb for the intensity of Israel's grief during times of severe tragedy. (See Jeremiah 6:26 and Amos 8:10.)

Second, Zechariah compared this time of mourning to that "at Hadad Rimmon in the plain of Megiddo" (Zech. 12:11). Although Hadad Rimmon's location is not identified in Scripture, most commentators consider it modern Rummaneh, a village near the ancient city of Megiddo. It was at Hadad Rimmon that righteous King Josiah was mortally wounded, whereupon Judah greatly mourned his death (2 Chr. 35:23–25). Zechariah compared Judah's mourning for Josiah with the intense mourning the nation will experience when it sees its rejected and pierced Messiah at His Second Coming.

Third, the remaining verses in this chapter express how extensive and exclusive the Jewish repentance will be when, without exception, "every [Jewish] family" will mourn over its sin (Zech. 12:12). Four men are mentioned as representing various groups of mourners: David, Nathan, Levi, and Shimei (vv. 12–13). David represents the royal family; Nathan represents either the royal family or the prophetic line; and Levi and Shimei represent the priestly family. In that day, all individuals of "all the families that remain" (v.14)—that survive the Great Tribulation—will mourn privately over their sin.

Whether Jewish or Gentile, one need not wait to repent over sin. Redemption and reconciliation are possible this very moment. And the one who makes this commitment will find peace and purpose and experience eternal life to come.

CHAPTER 15

Israel's Defilement Removed

Zechariah 13:1–9

In the previous chapter, we saw God pour out His grace on Israel, resulting in the nation's redemption, its reconciliation to God, and its renewed covenant relationship with Him. In chapter 13, Zechariah revealed how the Holy Spirit will bring national cleansing to a redeemed Israel.

Israel's Cleansing

Zechariah declared, "In that day a fountain shall be opened for the house of David and for the inhabitants of Jerusalem, for sin and for uncleanness" (13:1). The fountain of cleansing is the shed blood of the pierced Messiah (12:10). Like a fountain that gushes forth a continual provision of water, so the Messiah's blood has been available to cleanse all individuals from sin, guilt, and moral defilement since the first century.

The word *sin* in verse 1 refers to "missing the mark," or failing to meet God's righteous moral standard. *Uncleanness* speaks metaphorically of ritual impurity associated with a woman's monthly cycle. Both terms aptly represent Israel's judicial guilt and defilement. This cleansing will take place at the Messiah's Second Advent.

The "house of David" and the "inhabitants of Jerusalem" are singled out as beneficiaries. Israel's cleansing will be total, covering the kingly line of David and the commoners as well.

Idolatry Cut Off

When the Messiah returns, God will remove all idolatry and abolish even the idols' names so that they will be remembered no more: "I will cut off the names of the idols from the land, and . . . I will also cause the prophets and the unclean spirit to depart from the land" (v. 2). The unclean spirits are demonic agents or spirits that energize false prophets to speak and commit evil acts; they will also be cut off.

If any false prophet refuses to heed God's warning to stop prophesying, his parents will execute him, as prescribed in the Mosaic Law. His father and mother will say to him, "'You shall not live, because you have spoken lies in the name of the LORD.' And his father and mother who begot him shall thrust him through when he prophesies" (v. 3). In other words, honor for God's name and love for truth will transcend the most intimate relationships, even a parent's love for a son.

The Mosaic Law commanded parents to kill their evil sons by stoning them; but in the Day of the Lord, these sons will be stabbed to death. The word for "thrust" (Hebrew, *daqar*) is the same word used for "pierce" in Zechariah 12:10, where God said, "they will look on Me whom they pierced."

On threat of death, false prophets will quickly deny involvement in such evil practices: "And it shall be in that day that every prophet will be ashamed of his vision when he prophesies; they will not wear a robe of coarse hair to deceive" (13:4). Shame and fear of death will compel them to stop all prophesying. The genuine prophet often wore "a robe of coarse hair" to distinguish him as a prophet, in keeping with his frugal lifestyle and mournful pronouncements. (See 1 Kings 19:13, 19; 2 Kings 2:8, 14; Matthew 3:4.) Fearful of detection, the masquerading prophet will discard the mantle he wore to deceive people, covering up his activities.

Zechariah described the false prophet's deception and defense: "But he will say, 'I am no prophet, I am a farmer; for a man taught me to keep cattle from my youth'" (Zech. 13:5). This means he literally will say, "A man bought or possessed me, and I have been made a bondsman from my youth." To hide his involvement, he will claim to have been sold into slavery while young and taught to farm by his master. Thus the man will claim to be a slave of the lowest class, controlled by his master and never able to acquire the knowledge or ability needed to be a prophet. Discerning individuals who know him will detect his deception. Wounds on the man's body will give him away. He will be asked, "'What are these wounds between your arms [breast]?' Then he will answer, 'Those with which I was wounded in the house of my friends'" (v. 6).

Some believe the phrase *wounded in the house of my friends* is a Messianic prophecy referring to the piercing of Messiah's hands. However, this view is untenable. First, the Messiah was never wounded in the house of His friends but by Roman executioners who had no relationship with Him. Second, He was never wounded many times in His breast, as indicated in verse 6, but in His hands. Third, Messiah was not, nor would He ever claim to have been, a slave to any man on Earth. Fourth, the Messiah was never questioned by people of the world concerning His wounds after His resurrection. Fifth, the Messiah was a carpenter, not a farmer. Sixth, the Messiah was a prophet and never denied it. Seventh, the sequence of events presented in this chapter does not coincide with the time of the Messiah's crucifixion.

Those interrogating the man in Zechariah 13 know he is lying. Moreover, his wounds are self-inflicted, given to himself while practicing idolatry. Like the prophets of Baal, he cut his body, hoping to propitiate or placate false gods (cf. 1 Ki. 18:28). These types of lesions characterized many idolatrous men in that day, especially Canaanites. In Israel, priests and prophets were continually warned against such practices (Dt. 14:1).

Infliction of Christ

Abruptly, the Lord's focus shifts from the false prophet's inflictions to the infliction of the true Shepherd who was smitten for the sins of God's people: "Awake, O sword, against My Shepherd, against the Man who is My Companion,' says the LORD of hosts. 'Strike the Shepherd, and the sheep will be scattered; then I will turn My hand against the little ones'" (Zech. 13:7). This verse covers a lengthy period, from Christ's crucifixion through the Great Tribulation.

The Shepherd. The Messiah is the righteous Shepherd. God the Father called Him "My Shepherd" and "My Companion." The word *shepherd* is related to the word used in Zechariah 11:4–17 and refers to the one who was pierced in Zechariah 12:10—Jesus the Messiah.

The word *companion* (Hebrew, *amit*) speaks of a human being who is associated in a family connection; in this context, he must be closely united or joined to God the Father. Thus He is a human being in an equal relationship with God. This word clearly refers to Jesus the Messiah, who is both human and divine. This truth is both awe-inspiring and staggering, plainly teaching the Messiah's equality with God.

The Sword. The Redeemer is smitten: "Awake, O sword, . . . [and] strike the Shepherd." The word *sword* pictures an instrument used by a judicial authority to inflict death and is a symbol of God's divine wrath. This is not man's wrath being inflicted on the Messiah, but God's righteous wrath being poured out on Him who bore the sins of the world upon Himself and shed His blood for the remission of sin.

God the Father commanded the sword to arise and carry out divine justice. The command indicates it was God's will that Jesus be smitten. Although wicked men murdered Him, His death nevertheless was predetermined by the counsel and divine plan of Almighty God, who ordained that Messiah would die for the sins of the world (Acts 2:23). The sword of divine justice did not fall on a wicked man but on a righteous Messiah who is the Son of God. He is the same Lamb of God who was pierced for the sins of humankind (12:10; cf. Isa. 53:5). Isaiah prophesied that it pleased God the Father to bruise the Messiah and "make His soul an offering for sin" (Isa. 53:10).

The Sheep. The sheep that reject the Shepherd are scattered. Those who fled the smitten Shepherd were the Jewish people at His crucifixion. The Lord predicted that His disciples would flee then (Mt. 26:31). But their scattering was not the complete fulfillment of this prophecy; the prophecy also involves the nation of Israel. Its scattering took place in A.D. 70 with the Roman destruction of Jerusalem, and again in A.D. 135 when the Romans put down the Bar Kokhba revolt against Roman occupation and rule in Jerusalem. After the revolt, Jewish people were scattered across the earth in what is commonly called the Diaspora.

The phrase *then I will turn My hand against the little ones* has been interpreted in various ways (Zech. 13:7). Some teach that God has turned away from His anger against the sheep to show them mercy, love, and grace. We would like to embrace this position, but the context does not support the interpretation. This expression is to be interpreted in a punitive sense and does not suggest God showing mercy to a faithful remnant of Jewish people. Jewish people have suffered 2,000 years of persecution and are yet to face the greatest holocaust of their history during the Great Tribulation (Jer. 30:7; Rev. 12:1–17): "And it shall come to pass in all the land,' says the LORD, 'that two-thirds in it shall be cut off and die, but one-third shall be left in it'" (Zech. 13:8).

During the Great Tribulation, two-thirds of the Jewish population will perish. This percentage is high because (1) Satan will try to annihilate Israel (Rev. 12), (2) the false prophet will kill Jewish people who refuse to worship the Antichrist (13:15), and (3) many will die during the invasion of Jerusalem (Zech. 14:1–3).

However, chapter 13 ends with a glorious prediction:

I will bring the one-third through the fire, will refine them as silver is refined, and test them as gold is tested. They will call on My name, and I will answer them. I will say, "This is My people"; and each one will say, "The LORD is my God" (v. 9).

God promises the redemption of a righteous remnant in Israel that will survive the refining furnace of the Tribulation. As silver and gold are tried in the fire, so will the Great Tribulation purge away all of Israel's iniquity. This repentant remnant will emerge from its experience free of sin. With its suffering finally over, Israel will be established in its land to enjoy all of the blessings promised in the New Covenant (Ezek. 36:25–38). Both Hosea and the apostle Paul foresaw this great day as well (Hos. 2:23; Rom. 11:26–27).

God will acknowledge the redeemed, refined remnant when He says, "This is My people," whereupon the people will respond, "The LORD is my God" (Zech. 13:9). What a wonderful day awaits Israel when the Messiah brings a redeemed and cleansed remnant to complete salvation!

CHAPTER 16

The Messiah's Glorious Return
Zechariah 14:1–7

Zechariah closed his prophetic predictions with a sweeping overview of Israel's future. The prophet described three major events that will take place: (1) a future invasion of Jerusalem during the Great Tribulation, (2) the destruction of the Gentile invaders at the Messiah's Second Advent, and (3) the establishment of God's Millennial Kingdom. After the Lord's return, Jerusalem will be exalted and become the center of worldwide worship. These prophecies presuppose Israel's existence as a sovereign nation in the last days.

This chapter focuses on God's plan for an elect, preserved, and redeemed Israel. God has not forsaken the covenants He made with the Jewish nation and will bring to fruition everything He has ordained for the Jewish people.

The Massive Attack

Zechariah's prophecy begins with a description of Jerusalem's suffering in the Day of the Lord:

> Behold, the day of the LORD is coming, and your spoil will be divided in your midst. For I will gather all the nations to battle against Jerusalem; the city shall be taken, the houses rifled, and the women ravished. Half of the city shall go into captivity, but the remnant of the people shall not be cut off from the city (Zech. 14:1–2).

The time is the seven-year Tribulation, also called "the time of Jacob's trouble" (Jer. 30:7). Near the midpoint of the seven years, a huge army from the north, south, and east will try to capture and plunder Israel. It will be led by a leader called Gog from the land of Magog (Ezek. 38—39). The ruler will come from a land north of Israel, interpreted as Russia by conservative Bible commentators.

Russia will be joined by a number of nations from Southern Europe and a number of countries in the Middle East. Those confederated with Russia will be Persia (Iran), Ethiopia, Libya, Gomer, the people from Togarmah of the north, and many other people (38:5–6). This confederacy will invade Israel (v. 8) with the sole purpose of destroying it and plundering it for its great wealth (vv. 12–13). This army will be so vast that it will seem like a cloud with a shadow that covers the land (vv. 9, 16).

When God sees this huge army descend on little Israel, He will become furious; and in jealousy for the nation, He will pour out His wrath on Gog's army (vv. 18–19), destroying it with (1) an earthquake; (2) a spirit of confusion, causing it to self-destruct; (3) a major pestilence (disease); and (4) huge hailstones of fire and brimstone that rain down on the enemy, burying those who survived the other three manifestations of His wrath (vv. 20–22). The destruction will be so massive that it will take seven years to burn the weapons and seven months to bury the dead (39:9–12). Israel will not lift a finger to defend itself against Gog's invasion. Gog's army will be destroyed by a supernatural work of the Lord.

The purpose of the destruction of Gog's army is threefold: to preserve Israel from annihilation, to inform the nations that they will no longer be allowed to "profane [God's] holy name anymore" (v. 7), and to send a message to them that any future attempt to destroy Israel will end with their destruction (vv. 7–8).

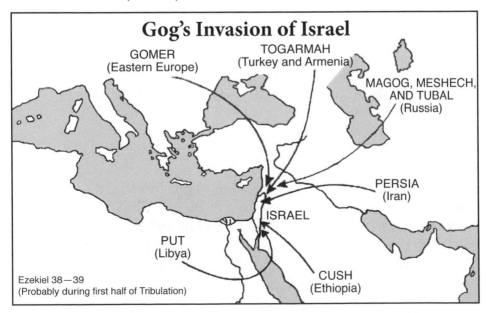

Gog's Invasion of Israel

GOMER
(Eastern Europe)

TOGARMAH
(Turkey and Armenia)

MAGOG, MESHECH, AND TUBAL
(Russia)

PERSIA
(Iran)

ISRAEL

PUT
(Libya)

CUSH
(Ethiopia)

Ezekiel 38—39
(Probably during first half of Tribulation)

The Tribulation closes with another attack on Israel. This invasion is commonly known as Armageddon (Joel 3:9–16; Rev. 16:14, 16; 19:11–19) and "the battle of that great day of God Almighty" (Rev. 16:14). All the armies of the world will converge on Israel at the end of the Great Tribulation in an attempt to destroy the Antichrist's rule and annihilate Israel.

Although Joel did not use the term *Armageddon,* he was one of the first prophets to foretell the details of this battle. He said the nations will beat their agricultural implements into weapons and assemble themselves in the Valley of Jehoshaphat. Today the Valley of Jehoshaphat is called the Kidron Valley and is located between the Temple Mount on the west and the Mount of Olives on the east.

Then the nations will gather in four major areas to do battle: The first is the Valley of Jehoshaphat. The second is Mount Megiddo (Hebrew, *Armageddon;* Rev. 16:16). The word *Armageddon* is made up of two Hebrew words: *har,* meaning "mountain," and *megiddo,* which means to "crush, kill, strike, massacre" (i.e., "mountain of destruction").

Megiddo is a mound that has been built up from the rubble of 20 cities for 3,000 years, reaching some 70 feet high. It is located at the southwest end of the Carmel mountain range bordering the Jezreel Valley and stretches 22 miles long and 16 miles wide. Megiddo is the crossroads of the Middle East, going north and south. Two major trade routes meet at the mount: the King's Highway and Via Maris ("way of the sea"). In 1799, Napoleon Bonaparte stood on Megiddo and called it a "natural battlefield."

The third area where the battle will take place is Edom (Isa. 34:6; 63:1–6), located southeast of Jerusalem. The fourth location is the entire country of Judah (Zech. 12:2–11; 14:2).

Although God said He will gather all nations to battle in Israel (Joel 3:2; Zech. 14:2; Rev. 16:16), the nations also will come of their own accord to overthrow the Antichrist (Dan. 11:40–44) who will have set himself up in Israel as a world ruler (Rev. 13:7), demanding all nations worship him as God (vv. 8, 12, 15). Amazingly, Satan will also gather the nations to Israel. Demonic spirits from Satan, the Antichrist, and the false prophet will draw the world's kings to war through the working of miracles (16:13–14). But why would Satan, who will be in control of Israel via the Antichrist, wish to bring the nations to Israel for battle? Notice, Satan is really drawing them "to the battle of that great day of God Almighty" (v. 14).

Satan will bring them to Israel for a number of reasons. First, he will have been cast out of heaven, meaning his access to God will be cut off (12:9; cf. Job 1:6–12). Second, he will know that time is running out for him, and he must act quickly to thwart God (Rev. 12:12). Third, he will want to pour his wrath out on Israel (v. 12), hoping its destruction will destroy God's program (vv. 6, 13, 15, 17). Fourth, he will try to destroy Christ at His Second Advent (Ps. 2:2–4), for if he can overthrow Christ's rule on Earth, he can keep Earth for himself (Rev. 16:14) and escape being destroyed by the Messiah.

With a prophetic eye, Joel saw into the future: he saw multitudes of soldiers stream into the Jezreel Valley, surging toward their destruction: "Multitudes, multitudes in the valley of decision! For the day of the LORD is near in the valley of decision" (Joel 3:14). The word *multitudes* comes from a root word in Hebrew (*hama*) that means "to make a loud noise" or "to be turbulent." The multitudes of troops will produce a deafening sound as they thunder into the valley of decision.

Scripture details the areas from which they will come. The king of the south, most likely Egypt's leader, will enter the land with a confederacy from North Africa (Dan. 11:40). The king of the north, possibly another confederacy headed by Russia (v. 40), will descend on Israel. The kings of the east will sweep across the dried-up Euphrates River (v. 44; Rev. 16:12) with 200 million men (Rev. 9:16) to join the other nations, and the armies of Western Europe will already be in the land, helping the Antichrist defend his holdings.

War will break out among the military factions. What many call the battle of Armageddon will not be a single battle but actually a war, for the word *battle* (Greek, *polemos*) means a "war" or "campaign" (16:14). The war is centered on Jerusalem (Zech. 14:2), but it will extend for a 200-mile radius around the city (Rev. 14:20).

Zechariah described this siege vividly. Jerusalem will be captured, houses will be ransacked and plundered, women will be violently raped, and half of the population will be exiled into slavery. Yet God will spare a remnant of Jerusalem's population from this massive destruction (Zech. 14:2). As previously mentioned, two-thirds of the Jewish people in Israel will die during this invasion, but one-third will be miraculously spared to enter the Millennial Kingdom (Zech. 13:8–9; Rom. 11:26). The one-third is a righteous Jewish remnant that survives the battle of Armageddon. God will supernaturally protect these Jews from annihilation by the Antichrist (Zech. 13:9; Rev. 12:14, 17).

The Messiah's Appearance

In Israel's darkest hour, when Jerusalem seems destined for destruction and the Jewish people destined for exile, the Lord will intervene. Said Zechariah: "The LORD will go forth and fight against those nations, as He fights in the day of battle" (Zech. 14: 3). The phrase *go forth* ("go out") is a technical term used for a king going to do battle with his enemy. The Lord is pictured as a warrior coming swiftly to Israel's side in order to defeat its enemies (Ex. 15:3; Isa. 42:13). If it were not for this promise, the small remnant left in Jerusalem might have despaired.

Joel mentioned the wonders that will take place in the heavens just prior to the Lord's coming in judgment: "The sun and moon will grow dark, and the stars will diminish their brightness" (Joel 3:15; cf. Mt. 24:29; Mk. 13:24–25; Rev. 6:12–13).

Awesome will be the appearance of the Lord! Suddenly, He will appear in the clouds; and the brightness of His glory will illumine the universe (Mt. 24:30). He is coming on a white stallion; and on His head will be many crowns (diadems), a symbol that He is the conquering King of kings (Rev. 19:11–12, 16). The crowns also denote His royalty and majesty as sovereign King and Lord of heaven and Earth.

His eyes will be a flame of fire, and His vesture will have been dipped in blood (vv. 12–13), a picture of His penetrating judgment on the nations. He will not come alone. The armies of heaven will follow Him—saints from throughout the ages and the angelic host of heaven (v. 14). They will ride on white horses and be clothed in fine linen, clean and white, symbolizing the righteousness of God. As a Warrior-King in battle array, the Lord is coming in righteousness to judge and fight the Antichrist, the false prophet, and all who follow them into battle against Israel (v. 11). He is coming to judge the rulers of darkness and reclaim Earth from Satan's control. The white horse symbolizes the Messiah's glorious victory over His enemies.

How will the armies that invaded Israel react at the Messiah's appearing? Wrote King David:

The kings of the earth set themselves, and the rulers take counsel together, against the LORD and against His Anointed [Messiah], saying, "Let us break Their bonds in pieces and cast away Their cords from us" (Ps. 2:2-3).

Their first response will be to fight Him in hopes of destroying Him, but they will be no match for the Lord. From His mouth will come a sharp sword that He will use to destroy them (Rev. 19:15). This sword refers to the Messiah's Word that proceeds from His mouth. As the Warrior-King, He will simply speak, and His Word will consume the Antichrist and his armies.

The apostle John told us the Messiah's "robe [is] dipped in blood" (v. 13). This is not His blood but the blood of His enemies. "He Himself [Messiah] treads the winepress of the fierceness and wrath of Almighty God" (v. 15; cf. Isa. 63:1–3).

The actual judgment will be poured out in the "valley of decision" (Joel 3:14). The Hebrew word for "decision" (*charute*) has a basic meaning of "to decide" and "to sharpen" or "to cut." Thus it is used metaphorically in reference to God's decision to cut these huge armies into pieces as one would mow down grain with a sharp threshing sledge.

God is longsuffering with people, "not willing that any should perish but that all should come to repentance" (2 Pet. 3:9). Yet human beings despise His goodness, forbearance, and longsuffering. So judgment must inevitably come (Rom. 2:2–6).

Joel pictured the nations as harvested for judgment: "Put in the sickle," he cried (Joel 3:13). In Revelation 14, John declared that the nations are ripe for judgment. He used two different Greek words for "ripe": one speaks of the grapes as overripe and starting to wither (v. 15), and the other refers to the grapes as full grown (v. 18), at their peak for harvesting. With the help of angels, Christ thrusts in the sharp sickle, cutting down the nations in judgment (vv. 14–16, 19).

Joel said the winepress was full and the vats overflowed with the harvest (Joel 3:13). The imagery portrays grapes being trampled underfoot until all of the juice is squeezed out to make wine. But here, blood, not grape juice, spurts from the winepress of God's wrath (Rev. 14:14–20). In the day of God's vengeance, the Lord's garments will be stained with the blood of those He has slain (Isa. 63:1–3; Rev. 19:13).

When the Lord speaks in judgment, the soldiers' flesh will be consumed from their bodies while they still stand (Zech. 14:12). The Hebrew word *consume* literally means "rot" and conveys the idea of wasting away, like the flesh of a leper. At Armageddon, the victims' flesh will decay rapidly from their bodies and fall off their bones, leaving only skeletons.

In other words, this massive army will seem like grapes crushed in a winepress after the Lord destroys it. The carnage will reach "up to the horses' bridles" (about five feet high) and cover an area "one thousand six hundred furlongs" (about 200 miles, Rev. 14:20). In contrast, the garments of God's armies will be spotless; Messiah alone will fight and gain this victory.

After the world's massive army is destroyed, an angel will cry out in a loud voice for all of the fowl that fly to come and devour the flesh of the men and animals that were destroyed by the Lord (19:17). At the call, vultures, which are voracious eaters, will descend swiftly on the carrion and devour it in minutes. They will eat the "flesh of kings, . . . captains, . . . mighty men, . . . horses and . . . all people, free and slave, . . . small and great" (v. 18). The Antichrist's army will include all classes of people, and it will be totally consumed. Seeing the ugly birds feed on the decaying carcasses of millions of men in a 200-mile radius of Jerusalem will be a terrifying spectacle beyond imagination.

Christ's appearance for the battle of Armageddon will affect people three ways:

> **(1) Visually.** They will not be able to see properly because darkness will envelop the universe immediately prior to the Lord's Second Coming (Mt. 24:29). Those who would not receive the light of God's Word, which provides salvation in Jesus Christ, will be left to grope in their darkness, only to be destroyed "with the brightness of His coming" (2 Th. 2:8).

> **(2) Auditorily.** They will not be able to hear properly. Their ears will be affected when "the LORD also will roar from Zion, and utter His voice from Jerusalem" (Joel 3:16). While men stagger around in a desperate search for light to relieve their blindness, they will be struck with terror as the Lord's voice rolls through the heavens like the roar of a lion that makes its presence known before devouring

its prey. Those who would not open their ears to hear the truth spoken by the 144,000 Jewish witnesses during the Tribulation (Mt. 24:14; Rev. 7) will be given a strong delusion that they should hear and believe Satan's lie (2 Th. 2:11). With the word of His mouth and the breath of His lips, Christ will slay the nations gathered for battle (Isa. 11:4; Rev. 19:15).

(3) Mentally. They will think the entire world is disintegrating. When Christ returns, His roar will shake "the heavens and earth" in judgment (Joel 3:16). Men will feel as if the foundation and framework of creation are being destroyed. The convulsing of nature will be a sign that God's day of grace and compassion on an ungodly rebellious world has come to an end; it will be the day of the Lord's judgment.

But what of the righteous in Israel who survive the Tribulation? "The LORD will be a shelter for His people, and the strength of the children of Israel" (v. 16). God will supernaturally protect a remnant of Jews from both the Antichrist and the judgment of Christ at His Second Coming (Zech. 13:9; Rev. 12:14, 17).

When Christ destroys Israel's enemies, the nation's eyes will be opened; and it will know that He has been its Messiah and Protector all along (Joel 3:17). When Christ dwells in the midst of Jerusalem, Israel will feel secure, knowing that His presence assures its safety from all future foreign aggressors (2:27; 3:17).

With world conditions as they are today, many people are asking, "Will the battle of Armageddon be a nuclear holocaust?" Nuclear weapons are being developed to such a degree that their limited use is feasible. One cannot rule out the possibility.

Remember, Armageddon will not be a single battle but, rather, a campaign of battles in which vast numbers of soldiers will be destroyed before the Lord returns to Earth. The culmination of the campaign will be the destruction of the world's armies in Israel by the Lord at His Second Coming (Rev. 19:15).

The Messiah's Arrival

When the Messiah intervenes militarily on Israel's behalf, His feet will touch the Mount of Olives:

And in that day His feet will stand on the Mount of Olives, which faces Jerusalem on the east. And the Mount of Olives shall be split in two, from east to west, making a very large valley; half of the mountain shall move toward the north and half of it toward the south (Zech. 14:4).

This earthquake is connected to the seventh bowl judgment in Revelation 16:18–19. The newly formed valley will enlarge Jehoshaphat's Valley where God will judge the Gentile nations that survive the Great Tribulation (Joel 3:2; Mt. 25:31–46).

Millennia ago, as the Lord ascended back to heaven after 40 days of postresurrection ministry, an angel prophesied that He would return in like manner to the same spot on the Mount of Olives (Acts 1:9–12). Note that these verses emphasize the physical, personal, public, literal, and visible return of the Messiah to Earth in His glorified body.

Zechariah continued: "Then you shall flee through My mountain valley, for the mountain valley shall reach to Azal. Yes, you shall flee as you fled from the earthquake in the days of Uzziah king of Judah" (Zech. 14:5). The split will create a massive valley running eastward to Azal. Although Azal's location is unknown today, it probably will mark the end of this newly formed valley east of Jerusalem.

Zechariah compared the earthquake's severity to an earthquake two centuries earlier, in King Uzziah's day (Amos 1:1). The future earthquake will produce a valley large enough to allow a remnant of Jewish people to flee from the holocaust taking place in Jerusalem.

A host of saints will accompany the Messiah on His return. Overjoyed at the prospect of His Coming, Zechariah cried out, "Thus the LORD my God will come, and all the saints with You" (Zech. 14:5). The saints are Old Testament believers (Dan. 12:1–2; Jude 14–15), Church Age believers (Rev. 19:8), and Tribulation believers martyred for their faith (7:13–14; 20:4). All will return in their glorified bodies, with the Messiah.

As stated earlier, just before the Messiah's return, phenomenal changes will occur in the heavens:

It shall come to pass in that day that there will be no light; the lights will diminish. It shall be one day which is known to the LORD—neither day nor night. But at evening time it shall happen that it will be light (Zech. 14:6–7; cf. Mt. 24:29).

The word *diminish* means to "thicken, congeal, or become dense." The celestial heavens will appear as dense, thick darkness immediately before the Lord returns. This day will be one of a kind; it will be difficult to distinguish between night and day. At "evening time," or the end of this period of darkness, light will reappear. The darkness will end with heaven's light being restored to an even greater intensity when the Lord appears. Matthew wrote, "Then the sign of the Son of Man will appear in heaven, . . . and they will see the Son of Man coming on the clouds of heaven with power and great glory" (Mt. 24:30). When the Messiah returns, His glory will light the heavens with greater intensity than has ever been seen on Earth.

The apostle John tells us that the Lord's return will be a worldwide event: "Every eye will see Him. . . . And all the tribes of the earth will mourn because of Him" (Rev. 1:7; cf. Mt. 24:30). Two groups of Earth dwellers will mourn: Those who are unsaved will intuit their destiny and mourn over their impending destruction, and Jewish people will instantly receive the Lord as their Messiah and mourn over their sins (Zech. 12:10–14).

Jerusalem has been "trampled by Gentiles" (Lk. 21:24) for centuries, but no more will strangers oppress her, for no unrighteous person will be allowed to defile Jerusalem after the Lord returns to establish His Millennial Kingdom (Rev. 21:3, 27).

The Messiah's glorious return will be a great day of rejoicing for Israel. In that day, Israel will experience redemption, victory over its enemies, and peace on earth.

The Times of the Gentiles

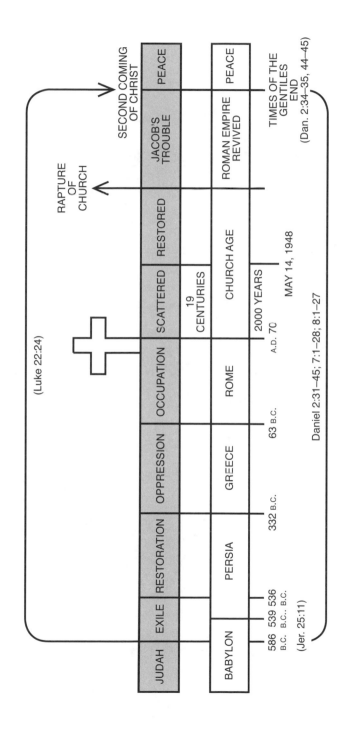

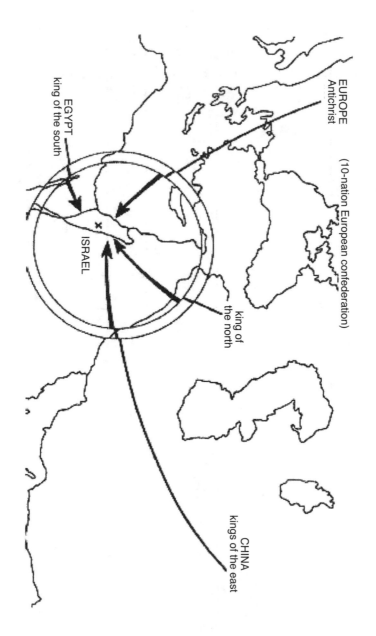

The Combatants of Armageddon

CHAPTER 17

Israel's Glorious Kingdom
Zechariah 14:8–15

The moment the Messiah's feet touch the Mount of Olives, an earthquake will flatten the land around Jerusalem and greatly elevate the city itself above the surrounding area. These topographical changes will radically alter Jerusalem's water situation.

The Mighty River

A mighty river will be created that flows from Jerusalem and feeds the entire Judean desert:

And in that day it shall be that living waters shall flow from Jerusalem, half of them toward the eastern sea and half of them toward the western sea; in both summer and winter it shall occur (Zech. 14:8).

This massive subterranean river will flow from Jerusalem into the Dead Sea to the east and the Mediterranean Sea to the west. The river will irrigate the desert surrounding the city, causing the Negev to blossom like a rose with foliage and produce (Isa. 35:1, 6). Many prophets foretold of the same event (Ps. 46:1–4; Ezek. 47:1–12; Joel 3:18).

According to Ezekiel, the river will flow from the Temple in Jerusalem, emptying into the Dead Sea and turning it into a freshwater lake that will produce a great multitude of fish, to the delight of fishermen (Ezek. 47:1–12):

Then he brought me back to the door of the temple; and there was water, flowing from under the threshold of the temple toward the east, for the front of the temple faced east; the water was flowing from under the right side of the temple, south of the altar. He brought me out by way of the north gate, and led me around on the outside to the outer gateway that faces east; and there was water, running out on the right side. And when the man went out to the east with the line in his hand, he measured one thousand cubits, and he brought me through the waters; the water came up to my ankles. Again he measured one thousand and brought me through the waters; the water came up to my knees. Again he measured one thousand and brought me through; the water came up to my waist. Again he measured one thousand, and it was a river that I could not cross; for the water was too deep, water in which one must swim, a river that could not be crossed.

He said to me, "Son of man, have you seen this?" Then he brought me and returned me to the bank of the river. When I returned, there, along the bank of the river, were very many trees on one side and the other. Then he said to me: "This water flows toward the eastern region, goes down into the valley, and enters the sea. When it reaches the sea, its waters are healed. And it shall be that every living thing that moves, wherever the rivers go, will live. There will be a very great multitude of fish, because these waters go there; for they will be healed, and everything will live wherever the river goes. It shall be that fishermen will stand by it from En Gedi to En Eglaim; they will be places for spreading their nets. Their fish will be of the same kinds as the fish of the Great Sea, exceedingly many. But its swamps and marshes will not be healed; they will be given over to salt. Along the bank of the river, on this side and that, will grow all kinds of trees used for food; their leaves will not wither, and their fruit will not fail. They will bear fruit every month, because their water flows from the sanctuary. Their fruit will be for food, and their leaves for medicine.

Although this is a physical river, it is called "living waters" because it will flow year round (Zech. 14:8). "Living water" is an Old Testament expression that refers to a flowing river in contrast to a stagnant one. During His ministry, Jesus gave the phrase spiritual significance when He used it to speak of the fullness of eternal life (Jn. 7:38–39), especially when dialoguing with the Samaritan woman (4:10, 14).

The Messiah's Rule

Zechariah continued: "And the LORD shall be King over all the earth. In that day it shall be—'The LORD is one,' and His name one" (Zech. 14:9).

When Jehovah establishes His earthly reign through the Messiah, Satan will no longer have any control as the "prince of the power of the air" (Eph. 2:2). Satan will be consigned to the bottomless pit. John wrote, "Then I saw an angel coming down from heaven, having the key to the bottomless pit and a great chain in his hand" (Rev. 20:1). A special place called "the bottomless pit" has been prepared for Satan and the demons (9:1–2, 11; 11:7; 17:8). This is not hell where the wicked dead reside, but a separate location of suffering.

Who is this angel? Some scholars have identified him as Christ, but there is no evidence to confirm this interpretation. The Lord has given this angel great authority to implement His mission. This authority is signified by a "key" to lock and unlock the abyss. The angel was given a "great chain" with which to shackle Satan and render him inactive for 1,000 years in the abyss.

The angel "laid hold of the dragon, that serpent of old, who is the Devil and Satan, and bound him for a thousand years" (20: 2). The angel strong-arms Satan, seizing and holding him firmly. Only God-given authority can subdue Satan. Then the angel "cast him into the bottomless pit, and shut him up, and set a seal on him, so that he should deceive the nations no more till the thousand years were finished" (v. 3). The incarceration, chaining, and sealing guarantee that Satan the dragon will be rendered incapable of deceiving mankind or interrupting the peace Christ promises in the Millennial Kingdom.

Peace will prevail on Earth, and Christ will rule with a rod of iron (19:15), allowing no wickedness.

Then Satan "must be released for a little while" (20:3) after the 1,000 years have run their course. Note that these thousand years are literal. This is not a symbolic use of a number, but a literal 1,000 years.

Messiah alone will take rightful rule over all of the earth and make the city of Jerusalem His capital. Jeremiah wrote, "At that time Jerusalem shall be called The Throne of the LORD, and all the nations shall be gathered to it, to the name of the LORD, to Jerusalem. No more shall they follow the dictates of their evil hearts" (Jer. 3:17).

The phrase *The LORD is one, and His name one* describes the Lord's universal rule and reign (Zech. 14:9). (See Zechariah 4:14; 6:5.) It does not mean Jehovah will possess things in the future that He has no control over today; He controls everything. But in the Millennium, Jehovah will be recognized as the one and only sovereign Lord.

The word for "one" in 14:9 is the Hebrew *echad*, which speaks of a unique oneness possessed only by Jehovah—the compound oneness of the triune God as expressed in the Shema: "Hear, O Israel: The LORD our God, the LORD is *one*!" (Dt. 6:4, emphasis added). The Shema embodies the very essence of Israel's covenant confession and faith, encapsulating Israel's faith in the monotheistic God.

In the Millennium, Jehovah will be universally recognized, accepted, and worshiped as the only unique, solitary, and incomparable God in the universe.[1] Never since the Fall of Man will people so recognize the triune God. There will be no ambiguity concerning whom humanity should believe in and worship. Notice that Zechariah does not refer to "our God" because Jehovah—the one and only true God—will be the one in whom all men and nations will believe.

As mentioned, Jerusalem and the surrounding area will be significantly altered at the Lord's return:

> All the land shall be turned into a plain from Geba to Rimmon south of Jerusalem. Jerusalem shall be raised up and inhabited in her place from Benjamin's Gate to the place of the First Gate and the Corner Gate, and from the Tower of Hananel to the king's winepresses (Zech. 14:10).

The city will be enormously elevated and expanded beyond its size and height today. Jerusalem, in all of its pristine beauty, will tower over the area and be visible from a great distance as people make their pilgrimages to it.

What will the area look like? First, the plain surrounding Jerusalem will reach from Geba of Benjamin, situated six miles to the northeast of Jerusalem (Josh. 21:17; 2 Ki. 23:8), to Rimmon in the southwest, situated 35 miles from Judah (Neh. 11:29). This plain is the Arabah, a flat valley about 100 miles in length that runs between the Dead Sea (1,300 feet below sea level) and the Gulf of Aqaba (300 feet above sea level), making

---

[1] F. Duane Lindsey, "Zechariah," *The Bible Knowledge Commentary*, eds. John F. Walvoord and Roy B. Zuck (Wheaton, IL: Victor Books, 1985), 1,570.

the Arabah the deepest valley on Earth.

During the Millennial Kingdom, Jerusalem will be rebuilt and greatly enlarged to adequately provide for the Messiah's capital, government, and new worship system. Zechariah envisioned a Jerusalem far larger than the Jerusalem of his day or even the city before its destruction by Babylon. In the Millennium, Jerusalem will extend from Benjamin's Gate on the north wall (the Gate of Ephraim mentioned in 2 Ki. 14:13) to the First Gate on the northeast corner, from the Corner Gate on the northwest corner to the Tower of Hananel (perhaps in the southeast corner) "to the king's winepresses" in the king's gardens south of the city near the Valley of Hinnom.[2] These dimensions give us, as they did the people of Zechariah's day, an indication of Jerusalem's size during the Messiah's rule on Earth.

The inhabitants of Jerusalem will live in safety and security: "The people shall dwell in it; and no longer shall there be utter destruction, but Jerusalem shall be safely inhabited" (Zech. 14:11). In other words, Jewish people living there during the Millennium will never fear destruction again:

> *No more shall an infant from there live but a few days,*
> *nor an old man who has not fulfilled his days; for the child*
> *shall die one hundred years old, but the sinner being one*
> *hundred years old shall be accursed. They shall build houses*
> *and inhabit them; they shall plant vineyards and eat their*
> *fruit. They shall not build and another inhabit; they shall*
> *not plant and another eat; for as the days of a tree, so shall*
> *be the days of My people, and My elect shall long enjoy the*
> *work of their hands. They shall not labor in vain, nor bring*
> *forth children for trouble; for they shall be the descendants*
> *of the blessed of the LORD, and their offspring with them.*
>
> *It shall come to pass that before they call, I will answer;*
> *and while they are still speaking, I will hear* (Isa. 65:20–24).

The Massacre Reviewed

In sharp contrast to the safety provided for the surviving Jewish remnant, annihilation is promised for Israel's enemies, who are under God's curse. Zechariah 14:12, like verse 3, speaks of the Lord fighting

---

[2] Walter C. Kaiser, Jr., *The Preacher's Commentary: Micah—Malachi* (Nashville, TN: Thomas Nelson Publishers, 1992), 23:439–440.

against the nations that invade Israel. In verses 12–15, Zechariah described how the Lord will defeat and destroy these nations at the time of Armageddon. Jehovah will annihilate Israel's enemies by three means: plague, panic, and power.

First, a plague will strike the invading armies:

> And this shall be the plague with which the LORD will strike all the people who fought against Jerusalem: Their flesh shall dissolve while they stand on their feet, their eyes shall dissolve [decay] in their sockets, and their tongues shall dissolve in their mouths (v. 12).

The words *plague* (Hebrew, *maggephah*) and *strike* (Hebrew, *magaph*) come from the same Hebrew root and mean to "strike" or "smite" with a supernatural pestilence—that is, to slaughter with divine judgment. People and animals within the enemy's camp are marked for destruction. The plague will fall "on the horse and the mule, on the camel and the donkey, and on all the cattle that will be in those camps. So shall this plague be" (v. 15).

Everyone who attacks Jerusalem will be eradicated because of God's curse. The plague will consume the enemy soldiers while they stand on their feet, leaving only skeletons. It will strike so quickly that those men's eyes and tongues will decay instantaneously, an indication of how rapidly this plague will kill the army in the moment of its victory.

Such destruction is not unlike what happened when the atomic bomb exploded over Hiroshima and Nagasaki, Japan. On August 6, 1945, the *Enola Gay*, a B-29 carrying the first atomic bomb, called "Little Boy," headed off early in the morning to attack the city of Hiroshima. It was learned later that the bomb killed more than 129,550 people in Hiroshima, some vaporized; and by year's end, over 100,000 more died from radiation and related disease. The energy and heat released from just one bomb burned right through many peoples' clothes, and the pattern of their clothes was emblazoned on their bodies.

A few days later, word came from Japan that almost all living things, human and animal, were literally seared to death. One can hardly imagine what it will be like when God speaks, and His Word consumes the army that comes to Israel at the battle of Armageddon.

Second, the Lord will send panic, or confusion, on the invading nations:

> It shall come to pass in that day that a great panic from the

LORD *will be among them. Everyone will seize the hand of his neighbor, and raise his hand against his neighbor's hand* (v. 13).

God will confound the armies that war against Jerusalem. The armies will panic and turn their weapons on each other; and in their madness, they will kill their own soldiers. As God confounded Israel's enemies to destroy themselves in the past, so will He do again (Jud. 7:22; 1 Sam. 14:20; 2 Chr. 20:23).

Third, God will give Judah power to destroy the armies that invade Jerusalem, and "Judah also will fight at Jerusalem" (Zech. 14:14). The Jewish remnant that initially escaped the invasion of Jerusalem through a valley divinely opened by Jehovah (vv. 4–5) will return to Jerusalem and kill the invaders who survive God's wrath during the campaign of Armageddon.

Once the invaders are dead, Israel will gather the wealth of the surrounding nations, "gold, silver, and apparel in great abundance" (v. 14). The spoils of war will be enormous.

The prophecies of Zechariah 14 are not presented in chronological order. Here is the proper order of their fulfillment:

> (1) All of the nations of the world will invade Israel in a campaign of battles culminating in what is commonly called Armageddon. Jerusalem will be captured, houses ransacked and plundered for spoil, women raped, and half of the population will be exiled into slavery (vv. 1–2).

> (2) At the Messiah's Second Coming, phenomenal changes will occur in the heavenly luminaries (vv. 6–7; cf. Mt. 24:29).

> (3) In Israel's darkest hour, the Messiah will appear and destroy the nations coming to war against it (Zech. 14:3). The armies will be destroyed by three means: a plague (vv. 12, 15); panic, causing them to turn on themselves (v. 13); and later by the divine power Israel will receive to annihilate those who remain. Israel then will gather the spoils of war (v. 14).

> (4) When the Messiah arrives, His feet will step on the

Mount of Olives, causing it to split apart and form a large valley that will allow a surviving remnant to escape the carnage in Jerusalem (vv. 4–5).

(5) A mighty river will flow from Jerusalem, watering the Negev and emptying into the Dead and Mediterranean Seas (v. 8).

(6) The Messiah will rule the earth from Jerusalem, and the city's inhabitants will live in safety forever (vv. 9–11).

(7) In the Millennium, nations will be required to appear in Jerusalem to worship the Lord and keep the Feast of Tabernacles (v. 16).

CHAPTER 18

Worship in the Kingdom

Zechariah 14:16–21

The Messiah's Second Coming is the dominant theme of chapter 14. His return will be sudden, unexpected, visible, personal, powerful, glorious, and triumphant. When He steps on the Mount of Olives, it will split apart (v. 4), altering the topography of Jerusalem and the surrounding area in preparation for the Kingdom. Peace will settle on the earth as Jesus the Messiah establishes His Kingdom reign and rule.

Zechariah's concluding section emphasizes that both holiness and worship will characterize and permeate Christ's Kingdom on Earth.

Reverence of Christ

Gentiles living in the Kingdom will be required to attend the Feast of Tabernacles in Jerusalem to worship the Lord:

And it shall come to pass that everyone who is left of all of the nations which came against Jerusalem shall go up from year to year to worship the King, the LORD of hosts, and to keep the Feast of Tabernacles (v. 16).

Who are these Gentiles required to attend the Feast of Tabernacles? They are the "sheep" that will be placed at Christ's right hand. After His return, Christ will judge the nations that survive the Great Tribulation to determine who from among the Gentiles will enter the Kingdom. (See Matthew 25:31–46.) This judgment of the nations (not to be confused with the judgment seat of Christ or the Great White Throne judgment) is mentioned in Matthew's Gospel:

When the Son of Man [Christ] comes . . . He will sit on the throne of His glory. All the nations will be gathered before Him, and He will separate them one from another. . . . And He will set the sheep on His right hand, but the goats on the left (25:31–33).

This judgment will take place in the Valley of Jehoshaphat between the Eastern Wall of the Temple Mount and the Mount of Olives (Joel 3:2, 12).

The "sheep" are redeemed Gentiles who will be placed at Christ's right hand, denoting a place of honor and blessing. They will inherit the Kingdom prepared for them from the foundation of the world. Evidence of their regenerated nature will be their kind treatment of the Lord's brethren, the Jewish people, during the Great Tribulation. These righteous Gentiles are amazed that Christ honors them for ministering to Jewish people during this time of Jewish suffering. Only redeemed Gentiles, along with redeemed Jews, will be allowed to enter the Kingdom (Mt. 25:33–40).

Unlike the "sheep," the "goats" are cursed and condemned to everlasting fire prepared for the Devil and his angels (v. 41). They, too, will be astonished at the Lord's verdict. He will inform them that their hostility toward and physical mistreatment of Jewish people during the Tribulation indicated they were unsaved (unregenerate). These unsaved Gentiles will be executed following this judgment (vv. 41–46). No unrighteous person will enter the Kingdom.

The redeemed Gentiles will make an annual pilgrimage to Jerusalem (the world's capital) to pray and "worship the King, the LORD of hosts" (literally, "Lord of armies," Zech. 14:16). The postexilic prophets used the phrase LORD of hosts to describe an all-powerful God who will accomplish what He decrees. Although no nation will maintain an army during the Millennial Kingdom, each nation will, however, still maintain its identity (Isa. 2:4; Mic. 4:3).

In that day, the world's population will worship "the Lord" as sovereign King over all the earth (Zech. 14:9). He will be loved and adored as the one and only true God. Gentiles who go to Jerusalem will grasp the corner of a Jewish priest's garment, wanting him to teach them God's Word (Isa. 61:6; Zech. 8:22–23).

Religious Celebration

Those coming to "worship the King, the LORD of hosts" (14:16) in the Millennial Kingdom will worship in a fourth Temple. It is commonly called the Millennial Temple (Ezek. 40—42). The Shekinah glory, which departed in the day of Ezekiel (10:3–5, 18–19; 11:23), will descend on this structure through the East Gate (43:1–5), making it a holy Temple.

During the Millennium, Sabbath worship will be reestablished, and animal sacrifice will be offered again (chap. 46). Bringing offerings to the Lord presupposes rebuilding the Temple and reinstituting the sacrificial system during the Millennial Kingdom. There are many similarities between the Aaronic and Millennial systems. In the Millennial system

- Worship centers on an altar (Ezek. 43:13–17) where blood is sprinkled (v. 18) and burnt, sin, trespass (40:39), and grain offerings (42:13) are presented.

- The Levitical order is reinstituted through the priestly ministry of Zadok (43:19).

- There are prescribed rituals of cleansing for the altar (43:20–27), the Levites who minister (44:25–27), and the sanctuary (45:18).

- New moon and Sabbath days will be observed (46:1).

- Morning sacrifices will be offered daily (v. 13).

- The feasts of Passover (45:21–24) and Tabernacles (v. 25) will be celebrated annually, along with the year of Jubilee at its proper time (46:17).

- There will be regulations to govern the manner of life, dress, and priestly order (44:15–31).

The Millennial Temple will be where this ministry will be performed and the glory of God will be manifested (43:4–5). Thus worship in the Millennium will bear a strong similarity to worship under the old Aaronic order.

Two questions arise concerning the Millennium's animal sacrifices.

(1) Since the priesthood was destroyed in A.D. 70, from where will the priests come who will lead in worship and offer sacrifices? The answer is that God will identify the true priests—the direct descendants of Aaron. Even though Jewish people today do not know what tribe they belong to, God does. He makes that clear when He seals 144,000 Jewish men (12,000 from each of the 12 tribes,

Rev. 7:4–8) during the Tribulation. Today it is believed that men with the last name of Levy are Levites, and men with the last name of Cohen are Levites who descended from Aaron. The name Cohen in Hebrew means "priest."

(2) If Jesus' sacrifice was the only efficacious, once-for-all sacrifice to expiate sin (Heb. 9:12), why will animal sacrifices that could never take away sin (10:4) be offered? It is true that the sacrifices in the Millennial Temple will not expiate sin, just as the Mosaic offerings could not. Many conservative commentators conclude that these offerings will be memorial in nature, similar to the church in this age keeping the Lord's Supper in remembrance of Christ's death. The offerings will be a visible reminder of Christ's efficacious work on the cross.

Although this is true, it would seem that the Millennial sacrifices will have an added function. They will be offered "to make atonement for the house of Israel" (Ezek. 45:17; see verses 15, 20). This is not a return to the Old Testament Mosaic Covenant or Law. It is an entirely new system set up by the Lord with dispensational distinctives that are applicable to the Millennial Kingdom. Remember, the Millennial system is based on the Abrahamic, Deuteronomic, and Davidic Covenants—not the Mosaic Covenant.

In the Old Testament, the word *atonement* means "covering." The Levitical system showed people the hideousness of their sinful condition and the need to cover their sins with a blood sacrifice. As mentioned previously, the blood atonement never took away sin. When the people made atonement, they were simply covering their sins, averting God's divine anger and punishment by paying a ransom. It was Christ's death on the cross, not the Levitical system, that made it possible for sins to be removed.

In like manner, the animal sacrifices offered during the Millennium will serve primarily to remove ceremonial uncleanness and prevent the Temple from being defiled. They will be needed because God's glorious presence will again dwell on Earth in the midst of sinful people. This purging act propitiates God, thus enabling Him to live among His people. The atonement cleansing was necessary in Leviticus because of the

Shekinah's presence in Exodus 40. The holy God had taken up residence in the midst of sinful, unclean people.

Similarly, Ezekiel foresaw the return of God's glory to the Millennial Temple. Uncleanness was treated as a contagion that had to be washed away or it would cause defilement. The future animal sacrifices will not deal with matters of eternal salvation but, rather, with the finite cleansing of impurities from people living in the Millennial Kingdom in their natural bodies. The Millennial Kingdom sacrifices will not diminish Christ's work on the cross or violate a literal interpretation of the sacrifices.[1]

Gentiles will come to Jerusalem to worship the Lord at the Feast of Tabernacles (Zech. 14:16). Two questions need to be addressed at this point: What is the Feast of Tabernacles, and why do the Gentiles go to Jerusalem to celebrate it?

The Feast of Tabernacles—or Ingathering, as it is sometimes called—is first mentioned in Leviticus 23:33–44. It is the seventh and final feast that Israel was commanded to keep and the third of three feasts that Jewish men were required to attend annually in Jerusalem.

In Hebrew it is called *Sukkot*, meaning "booths." It was named for the temporary huts that housed the Israelites during their 40 years in the wilderness (v. 42). The feast begins five days after the Day of Atonement (Yom Kippur), in September or October, and lasts for seven days, during which time Jewish people are supposed to dwell in booths they have constructed for the holiday. *Sukkot* is to be celebrated at the end of the growing season after the ingathering from the threshing floors and winepresses (Ex. 23:16; Dt. 16:13).

During the feast, three branches (palm, myrtle, and willow) are bound together in what is called a *lulav,* which is held in one's right hand. A citron, called an *etrog,* is held in one's left hand. A Jewish person then recites a blessing over his *sukkah* ("booth") on each of the seven days of the feast and waves the *lulav* in every direction.

In biblical times, the Feast of Tabernacles was a time of rest, praise, and giving of thanks. It was celebrated with great joy for the harvest of grain and wine gathered at year's end.

Why do redeemed Gentiles need to celebrate this feast in Jerusalem? First, the Lord commands them to do so. Second, it will be a joyful time

---

[1] Jerry M. Hullinger, "The Problem of Animal Sacrifices in Ezekiel 40–48," *Bibliotheca Sacra* 152, no. 607 (1995): 2–6.

of worship and praise to the Lord for the fruitful harvest He provides (cf. Amos 9:13). Third, it will also be a time when the world recognizes and worships Jehovah as King of the earth. In celebrating this festival, the nations will express their submission to Jehovah as the only true God of the universe.

Rain Control

Nations existing during the Kingdom Age will be required to send representatives to Jerusalem to worship the Lord at the Feast of Tabernacles. Those nations that fail to do so will pay dearly for their disobedience:

> *And it shall be that whichever of the families of the earth do not come up to Jerusalem to worship the King, the LORD of hosts, on them there will be no rain* (Zech. 14:17).

Lack of rain will bring hardship, and the entire world will know that the country disobeyed the Lord. When the Israelites refused to obey God's commandments, He punished them by withholding rain (Dt. 11:17; 28:23–24; 1 Ki. 17:1; Hag. 1:10–11).

Egypt is specifically singled out, should it not send representatives to the Feast of Tabernacles:

> *If the family of Egypt will not come up and enter in, they shall have no rain; they shall receive the plague with which the LORD strikes the nations who do not come up to keep the Feast of Tabernacles* (Zech. 14:18).

Why Egypt is specifically mentioned is not stated. Egypt is not dependent on abundant rain to water its crops because it draws water from the Nile River. Perhaps Egypt might think it would escape judgment. However, God has another judgment in store for the nation: It "shall receive the plague." Egypt knows what it means to experience plagues (Ex. 7:14—12:12, 29–30).

Prof. Eugene Merrill's comments are appropriate regarding God's punishment of both Egypt and the nations:

> *Egypt in the Bible is frequently a type of the world at large (Isa. 27:13; Rev. 11:8). Here, it is not distinguished, therefore, from the nations just mentioned but appears as a synonym for them. . . . Not only Egypt, but all the nations who do not go up to celebrate the Feast of Tabernacles will experience*

the severest repercussions. The prophet views this extreme measure not as a whimsical or arbitrary act of God but as a "punishment" (v. 19). The word here is literally "sin" . . . but by use of the metonymy of effect he speaks of the result in place of the cause. That is, the plague is the aftermath of sin in the sense that it is its punishment. The sin is of the most egregious kind, for in the covenant context of the passage it is nothing short of rebellion and repudiation of YHWH's dominion.[2]

Righteous Consecration

Only redeemed people—those made righteous through receiving Jesus the Messiah—will enter the Kingdom. Righteousness will prevail because Satan will be bound in the bottomless pit (Rev. 20:1–3), and the Lord will have cleansed the world of wickedness.

Holiness will characterize every aspect of the Kingdom, both secular and sacred. Zechariah emphasized this fact in the concluding verses of his prophecy:

In that day "HOLINESS TO THE LORD" shall be engraved on the bells of the horses. The pots in the LORD's house shall be like the bowls before the altar. Yes, every pot in Jerusalem and Judah shall be holiness to the LORD of hosts. Everyone who sacrifices shall come and take them and cook in them (Zech. 14:20–21).

The phrase *HOLINESS TO THE LORD* will be engraved or stamped on the most mundane objects, such as the bells on the horses and the pots and bowls used in the Kingdom Temple. The engraving will declare to all that the items are fit for Kingdom use. Everything used in the Kingdom administration will be considered holy to the Lord. Even the cooking utensils of people coming to Jerusalem to worship and study will be dedicated.

Zechariah closed his prophecy by saying, "In that day there shall no longer be a Canaanite in the house of the LORD of hosts" (v. 21). In biblical times, the word *Canaanite* referred to a person who was profane,

---

[2] Eugene H. Merrill, *An Exegetical Commentary: Haggai, Zechariah, Malachi* (n.p.: Biblical Studies Press, 2003), 318–319.

unclean, ungodly, or—with regard to merchants—dishonest. In Hosea 12:7, the word *Canaanite* was used of an Israelite who cheated in business. Canaanite practices were so wicked that God decreed the Canaanites' annihilation in order to rid the land of contamination. This type of person will forever be banished from the Kingdom.

Zechariah's name means "Jehovah remembers," a reminder that God will not forget His covenant commitment to Israel. The prophet Isaiah beautifully phrased God's everlasting love and commitment to His ancient people:

> *Can a woman forget her nursing child, and not have compassion on the son of her womb? Surely they may forget, yet I will not forget you. See, I have inscribed you on the palms of My hands; your walls are continually before Me* (Isa. 49:15–16).

Zechariah's prophecies reach far into the future. They are an ongoing testimony to Jewish people in every age that God does not forget His covenant promises to Israel. Zechariah's prophecy began with God's call for Israel to repent of its sin (Zech. 1:1–6), and it concludes with a promise of Israel's redemption, restoration, and return to righteous living. Jewish people can take hope and be assured that God will fulfill His covenant promises to Israel.

The 400 Silent Years

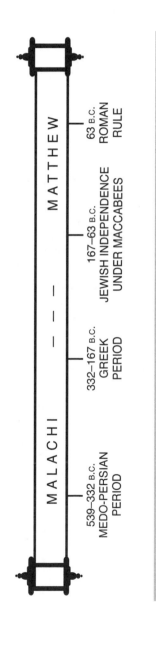

MALACHI — — — MATTHEW

539–332 B.C.
MEDO-PERSIAN
PERIOD

332–167 B.C.
GREEK
PERIOD

167–63 B.C.
JEWISH INDEPENDENCE
UNDER MACCABEES

63 B.C.
ROMAN
RULE

THE JEWISH PEOPLE AT THE MESSIAH'S FIRST COMING

POLITICALLY

- Ruled by Rome
- Looking for the Messiah
- Sanhedrin (local government in Israel) has limited power under Rome

RELIGIOUSLY

- Emphasis on religious externals
- Religious Groups:
  Pharisees – legalists, self-righteous
  Sadducees – free thinkers, worldly
  Essenes – mystic pietists, ascetics
  Believing Remnant – looking for the Messiah
- Talmud developed

General Index

Scripture Index

Recommended Reading

Baldwin, Joyce G. *Haggai, Zechariah, Malachi*. The Tyndale Old Testament Commentaries. Downers Grove, IL: InterVarsity Press, 1972.

Baron, David. *The Visions and Prophecies of Zechariah*. London, England: Hebrew Christian Testimony to Israel, 1916, 1951.

Boda, Mark J. *The NIV Application Commentary: Haggai, Zechariah*. Grand Rapids, MI: Zondervan, 2004.

Boice, James Montgomery. *The Minor Prophets*. Grand Rapids, MI: Kregel Publications, 1996.

Bullock, C. Hassell. *An Introduction to the Old Testament Prophetic Books*. Chicago, IL: Moody Press, 1986.

Feinberg, Charles L. *The Minor Prophets, Zechariah: Israel's Comfort and Glory*. Chicago, IL: Moody Press, 1976.

Freeman, Hobard E. *Introduction to the Old Testament Prophets*. Chicago, IL: Moody Press, 1968.

Hailey, Homer. *A Commentary on the Minor Prophets*. Grand Rapids, MI: Baker Books, 1972.

Hengstenberg, E. W. *Christology of the Old Testament: The Prophet Zechariah*. Grand Rapids, MI: Kregel Publications, 1970.

Hocking, David. *Visions of the Future: Studies in Zechariah*. Tustin, CA: HFT Publications, 2000.

Kaiser, C. Walter Jr. *The Preacher's Commentary: Micah, Nahum, Habakkuk, Zephaniah, Haggai, Zechariah, Malachi*, vol. 23. Nashville, TN: Thomas Nelson Publishers, 1992.

Keil, Carl Friedrich. *The Twelve Minor Prophets*, vol. 2. Trans. James Martin. Grand Rapids, MI: Eerdmans Publishing Company, 1954.

Laetsch, Theo. *The Minor Prophets*, reprinted. Grand Rapids, MI: Baker Books, 1950.

Laney, J. Carl. *Everyman's Bible Commentary: Zechariah*. Chicago, IL: Moody Press, 1984.

Lindsey, Duane F. *The Bible Knowledge Commentary: Zechariah*. Wheaton, IL: Victor Books, 1985.

McGee, J. Vernon. *Through the Bible with J. Vernon McGee: Proverbs—Malachi*, vol. 3. Pasadena, CA: Thru The Bible Radio, 1962.

Merrill, Eugene H. *Haggai, Zechariah, Malachi: An Exegetical Commentary*. Biblical Studies Press, 2003.

Meyer, F. B. *The Prophet of Hope*. Chicago, IL: Revell, 1900.

Pusey, E. B. *The Minor Prophets*, vol. 2. Grand Rapids, MI: Baker Books, 1950.

Robinson, George L. *The Twelve Minor Prophets*, reprinted. Grand Rapids, MI: Baker Books, 1952.

Stone, Nathan J. *Jehovah Remembers: Studies in Zechariah*. Moody Manna. Chicago, IL: Moody Bible Institute of Chicago, 1966.

Tatford, Frederick A. *The Minor Prophets*, vol. 3, reprinted. Minneapolis, MN: Klock & Klock Christian Publishers, 1982.

Unger, Merrill F. *Unger's Commentary on the Old Testament*, vol. 2. Chicago, IL: Moody Press, 1981.

_____. *Zechariah: Prophet of Messiah's Glory*. Grand Rapids, MI: Zondervan, 1963.

Willmington, H.L. *Willmington's Guide to the Bible*. Wheaton, IL: Tyndale House, 1981.

Other Books by David M. Levy

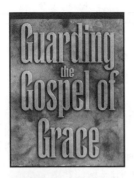

GUARDING THE GOSPEL OF GRACE
Contending for the Faith in the Face of Compromise
We often lack peace, joy, or victory in our walk with Christ because we're not clear how God's grace works in our lives. The books of Galatians and Jude are brought together in this marvelous work that explains grace, what can happen if you stray from it, and how to stay faithful.

JOEL: THE DAY OF THE LORD
What lies in store for the nations of the world? Learn what God has planned concerning the destiny of nations as they relate to Israel in the Day of the Lord. Illustrated chapter outlines and graphics give added insight into the timely and dynamic book of Joel, which surely is one of the most neglected and misinterpreted in the Bible.

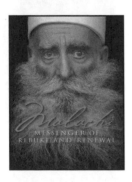

MALACHI
Messenger of Rebuke and Renewal
Whatever the need—social, political, or religious—you'll find the answer in this verse-by-verse, nontechnical exposition that deals with contemporary issues while providing a comprehensive chronology of Israel's prophetic history.

REVELATION
Hearing the Last Word
Why is there so much uncertainty and disagreement about the last days? What can we know about the Antichrist? What is the order of end-times events? What about Israel? What will life be like in the Millennial Kingdom? This valuable resource will help you know what to expect as Earth's final hour approaches.

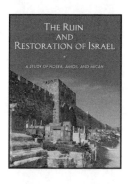

THE RUIN AND RESTORATION OF ISRAEL
A Study of Hosea, Amos, and Micah

An outstanding exposition that is as contemporary as today's news. Based on a literal-grammatical interpretation of Scripture, this book reveals the inerrancy of God's Word and shows how a covenant-keeping God chastens whom He loves but keeps His promises . . . forever.

THE TABERNACLE:
Shadows of the Messiah

Explore Israel's wilderness Tabernacle, the service of the priesthood, and the significance of the sacrifices. Excellent illustrations will open new vistas of biblical truth as ceremonies, sacrifices, and priestly service reveal the perfections of the Messiah.

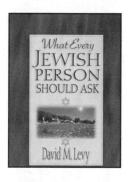

WHAT EVERY JEWISH PERSON SHOULD ASK

Can I know God? Why do I feel alienated from God? What can mitzvahs (good works) do for me? Is there really a Messiah? What decisions must I make about my spiritual life? If you need answers to life's most important questions, this excellent book is a must-read.

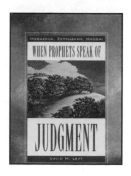

WHEN PROPHETS SPEAK OF JUDGMENT
Habakkuk, Zephaniah, Haggai

Is our nation on the brink of judgment? In this fascinating overview of Habakkuk, Zephaniah, and Haggai, you'll discover that the very conditions that led to Judah's downfall are all present in America today. This volume explores these conditions and challenges us to "redeem the time" as we move ever closer to the last days.

Zeill reveals Reo